BECOME THE ARCHITECT OF
YOUR BODY, MIND, AND SOUL

BECOME THE ARCHITECT OF YOUR BODY, MIND, AND SOUL

Lara Alexiou

Cover Photo Courtesy of Alex Cena.

ISBN: 1548298166
ISBN 13: 9781548298166

To all the seekers: May you discover that the answers are within.

TABLE OF CONTENTS

INTRODUCTION: THE YIN AND YANG OF TRANSFORMATION

"It is Yin and Yang. Light is the left hand of darkness... how did it go? Light, dark. Fear, courage. Cold, warmth. Female, male. It is yourself... both and one. A shadow on snow."

—URSULA K. LEGUIN

As A YOGA instructor, studio owner, and business mentor, the topic of personal happiness permeates many of the teachings I come across, and many of the questions I get from students.

Sometimes it seems as if we are all expected to be happy all the time as if happiness is the *one* great goal of life, and experiencing unhappiness, disappointment, or regret makes us failures.

Students and clients confide in me their feelings of guilt or shame when they feel unhappy about a situation. I hear things like, "I know this shouldn't bother me but..." If anyone has ever remembered saying this, then finding a quick recovery is essential.

Taoist philosophy teaches that emotions are energy in motion. *E-Motion.* Emotions are not static; they have a never-ending tide of ebb and flow. Nothing, including feelings, is permanent. All things end.

I have experienced this over and over in all aspects of my life: romantic relationships, business, health, and friendships. Passion burns up and out. Revenue goes up and down. Students commit and quit. Staff members come and go. Health—good and bad—can turn in the blink of an eye. One of the main things I have learned through the practice and teaching of yoga is not to resist these inevitabilities. Now, when they appear, I run out to meet them. Every day is an opportunity, and in times of strife I am led to discover the answer to this important question: How quickly can I recover?

Recovering in the face of adversity determines success in life. This is the gift of Yin and Yang. An experience only exists because of its opposite. It is only in darkness that light is revealed. The downs in life create the ups. When we can look courageously into the eyes of our deepest despair, we will see it reflects our greatest joys.

Life is a heartbeat, a series of ups and downs. We must embrace this truth because without this, we are left with a living death—a life of mediocrity at best, and at worst, despair. Since death comes to us all in time, let us really live life while we can, the best we can, and as fully as we can.

This book is about discovery, about applying simple tools *consistently* to reveal ever more truth about us. Together we will explore these techniques while embracing life's ups and recovering from life's downs with grace. We will find the paths to recovering as quickly as possible so we can move forward to our next adventure being a little wiser and a lot more comfortable with who we are and what we do. We will practice riding the waves of Yin and Yang.

CHAPTER 2

WHEN THE IMPOSSIBLE BECOMES POSSIBLE

"Nothing is impossible, the word itself says 'I'm possible'!"

—AUDREY HEPBURN

THE EASTERN HEALING Arts teach that movement and the physical body are the easiest tools to calm and focus the mind. When the body is in distress, discomfort or dis-ease, the mind is turbid and has difficulty staying in the present moment. Nothing pulls us out of the moment like physical pain. Discomfort in the body leads to a preoccupied mind and ultimately a dampened spirit. Our bodies really are temples, temples of our own making. We are the architects who design and build for ourselves strong and supple bodies. We have the power to create bodies that we find beautiful, bodies we respect, bodies that are welcoming places for our souls to reside.

My journey with yoga began when I noticed I was feeling *crowded* inside myself. I knew I needed to get my body moving, so I decided to give yoga a try. Maybe hot yoga was the answer to the questions my body seemed to be asking. I know now that this *crowdedness* I was experiencing was more than just a sign from my body. My very spirit was shouting out, asking for more space to grow, expand, and help me manifest my best work here in the world.

But the physical form is easier to hear than the spirit. That is why the body is such a great tool for spiritual transformation. We are more likely to respond to changes we can see, and I noticed physical transformation almost immediately. Sometimes my students see my postures and my practice, and believe I have always been at the level I am today. I constantly remind them that I began just like everyone else, out of touch with my body, including my toes! I did not waltz into the hot room and immediately drop into a perfect backbend. I could not hold a balancing pose for more than a few seconds. I did not even know how to breathe correctly! Regular, committed practice, coupled with a belief that I could improve, and a desire to do and be my best made me what and how I am.

When I first started practicing yoga, I remember seeing the other yogis in the room and thinking I would never be able to do that. I remember the yogis who looked at ease, comfortable in their bodies, and effortless when they performed what looked like amazing physical feats. I was wowed. I felt so far away from ever being able to move the way they were moving.

That is when the first lessons and the initial voice of my spirit began to whisper in my ear. We imagine our physical form to be fixed. Yoga taught me that this belief simply is not true. With practice and intention, I glimpsed the potential of my physical form and saw it was so much greater than I could have imagined. As my body changed, my mind and spirit also changed.

Through yoga, I unlocked not only the physical strength and flexibility but also the mental focus and peace of mind. My yoga practice shifted my entire inner perspective, my life, and how the two interact. Every physical impossibility that melted away inside the yoga room gave life to the thought that maybe the obstacles I faced outside of the practice room could be overcome as well. As excited as I was to be using my body in a way I never dreamed possible, I learned that the physical practice of yoga—*asana*—was not about perfecting my posture. Practicing the postures is about taking this very tangible aspect of yoga and applying the principles in every area of my life.

We are not just a body, after all. And most of our problems exist inside our heads and our hearts. How we think and how we feel determine what we do, and our thoughts create our reality.

We are all comprised of three forms of energy: Jing, Qi, and Shen. Jing is the physical form while the Qi is the life force that can either radiate within us or stagnate and rot. And Shen is Spirit, the part of us that is not our body, not our breath, not our thoughts, or emotions. In other words, Shen is the Soul.

When one of these energies changes, they all change. So if we can change our bodies, which seem immobile and solid, imagine how quickly we can change our minds or upgrade our life force energy! We should take a moment here to allow this to really sink in.

We can change our minds in an instant. We can be a hundred places in our minds in the blink of an eye. We entertain tens of thousands of thoughts and possibilities each day. It takes much longer for our physical forms to catch up. When transformation of our physical forms becomes a reality, we understand how easily we can change our minds, reignite our energy, and transform our lives.

This one realization changed my life. We are not carved from stone. We are living and breathing and continuously renewing ourselves. With each cellular turnover, infinite possibilities abound. This has proven true for me time and again over the years in my yoga practice and in my health. When I was twenty-five years old, I was diagnosed with Multiple Sclerosis—MS—an autoimmune disease that causes the body to attack itself affecting the brain and the spine. MS has no known cause and no known cure, and I was told I would be on medication for the rest of my life. But my belief in my body's ability to change, to adapt, to heal through my yoga practice, which specifically helps heal the spine, kept me showing up on the mat even on days when my energy was so low I could do little else. There were days I could not make it into work because my body was too weak and my mind too foggy, but I made it to yoga class. I knew on an intuitive level that yoga was helping me, and I knew that stopping my practice would hurt me.

Eventually, my yoga practice made a believer out of my very reputable, very non-Eastern physician. I have been asymptomatic now for thirteen years, and I no longer take any medication. These are things I was told were, for me, impossible.

When you can make the impossible happen within your body, you see the endless possibilities for your energy and spirit to follow. You are empowered to change your life and live your dreams. The impossible really does become possible through yoga!

CHAPTER 3

NEW CHALLENGES: STEPPING INTO THE UNKNOWN

"If there's a book that you want to read, but it hasn't been written yet, then you must write it."

—TONI MORRISON

IN 2014, I was asked to participate in the *Revitalize This!* Scranton's first TEDx Talk. I admit I was only vaguely familiar with TED Talks and had no idea that TEDx events were the local versions of these talks. I was, in fact, not at all sure what I had agreed to! As I did my research, what really struck me was that TED Talks are not only "ideas worth spreading," but also touted as the "talk of your life!"

Thankfully, I had some parameters to follow. Most of the participants in the event were either architects by profession or directly related in community building through the use of physical spaces. I was a yoga teacher and owned a yoga studio. I was not sure what I had to offer so I expressed my concern. The TEDx event organizers assured me that they were aware of this and wanted me to bring a different perspective to the evening.

Knowing that everyone understood I would not be speaking about architecture in the literal sense of homes or office space, I went to work creating my talk. TED does a great job walking its speakers through the process by offering guidelines, dos and don'ts, and support every step of the way. Writing my eight-minute talk (it can be up to eighteen minutes, but we were asked to keep it about ten minutes) was more challenging than writing this entire book! The irony here was that at the time, I had no idea that my TEDx Talk would evolve into the foundation for my first book. Back then, what I knew was this: I was seizing an opportunity to stretch beyond my perceived limits. And that is precisely one of the great lessons of yoga.

As I wrote my TEDx Talk, I trashed draft after draft, and almost gave the whole thing up. One particularly discouraging night when I told my husband Yanni that I just could not do the talk, he said, "Okay, you don't have to do it. Call them and tell them you're dropping out."

Well, of course I never made that call! My breakthrough moment came after realizing I could choose to back out, or I could choose to talk about my personal journey, the journey no one except my closest loved ones had heard. The title of my TEDx Talk, "Architecture of The Body, Mind and Soul," came to me as I reflected on how yoga and my other Eastern Healing Arts' practices helped me reshape myself physically, mentally, emotionally, and yes, spiritually. I had to be willing to *come out* as a spiritual being that inhabits a physical body. I was terrified. I was not even certain I would be allowed to use the word *Soul*. And I was scared of what I was putting out there—probably scared of rejection, of really being seen, and of being labeled in some way. My community is small and tight-knit. My husband and I are visible, respected, award-winning business people. Could I allow the intelligentsia community to see me holistically? Would I actually be willing to claim my physical *and* spiritual transformation?

Another thing most people, even those who knew me well, did not know about me was that I had been diagnosed with MS. Therefore, they knew nothing of my somewhat miraculous journey to remission. When I say most, I mean apart from my immediate family and a handful of close friends, I never talked about this with *anyone*. In some ways, my approach to the MS diagnosis was a combination of refusing to empower the disease, turning to the solution, and denying that this disease would take hold and limit my life. By not talking about MS, I made MS less real for me. This TEDx Talk was bringing this little known fact about me to light for others, while confronting me with its reality. I mention this because many people are dealing with chronic disease, either personally or within their families, and the truth is, some diseases are more socially accepted than others.

When I was diagnosed, very few people even knew what MS was or what a diagnosis meant; therefore, I had to educate anyone with whom I shared this information. Since I was having difficulty just walking down the street, talking to someone like this took more energy than I had. It became easier to hide and not discuss it at all.

Another tough thing about it is that most of us look fine. And some days we feel great and energized and can fully participate in our lives. But when we are having a bad day, it can be hard to explain to people because everyone's experience of MS is different. There are no *stages* like there are with cancer, for example, where people have a basic understanding of the different progressions of the disease and of the prescribed treatments and side effects. With MS, everyone's experiences of the symptoms, progress, and treatment is vastly different.

It also affects a young population. While anyone can be affected, the majority are young women. I was twenty-five. I was practicing yoga. I looked totally normal and maybe even a little more athletic or stronger than most because of my daily practice. People could not understand my fatigue, the balance issues, the medications, and the side effects. It was too much to explain, and I did not have the energy.

What I take away from my experience is that we never know what someone else is going through. We should not judge when a perfectly *normal* person has a handicapped license plate and parks close to an entrance. Riding the metro in DC, I never gave up my seat because I could not stand up for the long ride. We never know what someone else is dealing with.

I also did not like to talk about it because I was afraid of being labeled and of opportunities being taken away from me. I was afraid of labeling myself too. I was in my mid-twenties, a time of growing independence, of taking risks, of new job opportunities, new friends, and relationships, and I did not want anyone stopping me or suggesting that I was overdoing it.

I just kept moving forward with my life full force. I did not worry as much about the *how*. I focused on the *what*. I wanted to complete my intensive and physically demanding Bikram Teacher Training across the country—away from my family, friends, and doctors—just months after my diagnosis. I did not see how I was going to make it, but I had my heart on the end result and took each day breath by breath.

For those of us who are dealing with any kind of chronic issue, we are often unaware of the possibilities. People who have never been afflicted with chronic disease have a hard time understanding the unrelenting daily challenges involved such as pain, exhaustion, medication, and constant doctors' appointments. I write this not to complain but to explain. For me, treating MS involved daily injections for nine years. But I reached a point where I could not do that anymore. I sat down with my doctor to carefully weigh my options. My doctor told me health professionals know that MS sufferers do better when they start drug therapy immediately upon becoming symptomatic. We did that. But my doctor had no idea what might happen if I were to cease the daily injections. "We are moving into the unknown," he said.

As I mentioned earlier, I am happy to report I have been asymptomatic for thirteen years and free of medication for six years now. I was never told this was a possibility. Until I broached the subject, it was *not* a possibility. But I had been living with the diagnosis for years, while visualizing the life I wanted, working towards it, and living it every day.

I want to stress that I was able to let go of medication, but I did so only with my physician's approval. If you are dealing with any health issues, make sure you consult your health care professionals before changing any treatment protocols. It is important to avail yourself of every possibility and wellness tool. I believe yoga will help with *everything*, but yoga may not be the *only* thing you need. I would never advocate taking matters into your own hands without medical supervision.

What I do advocate is advocating for yourself. Sometimes the solutions are not presented simply because they have not been requested. First, ask yourself what is possible, and then ask for help in making the best possibilities your reality. Do not let anything stop you from dreaming and going out in the world to do your work. By living the best life possible, you help others do the same thing.

CHAPTER 4

HOW I GOT MY GROOVE BACK

"Don't settle for a relationship that won't let you be yourself."

—OPRAH WINFREY

I WAS REMINDED recently that sometimes we fall into a rut, and instead of climbing out of the rut, we grow comfortable in it. We actually forget we are in a rut. We decorate the rut. How often have we stayed in a situation that seems okay, but not great—a situation that, in hindsight, we see was a rut? I am finished decorating ruts!

I was in a romantic relationship for way too long that was, at best, mediocre. I count this as my deepest regret, staying in that rut. I am so grateful for my life today, for my wonderful, loving husband. I am thankful for good health, strong ties to my family, and a rewarding business with wonderful mentors, teachers, and students. My gratitude for my life now is what saves me from the depths of regret for staying in a rut—the wrong relationship—for so long.

It was hard to break free of the chains I forged for myself. On looking back, I now see that part of my problem was the absence of any long-term goals. I used every ounce of my energy to tread water each day merely to stay afloat. I never looked around to see where I was going or where I had come from or even what else was possible.

When I began working with my business mentor in 2009, my main objective was to open up my long-term thinking and set long-term goals. I was so focused on the day-to-day in all aspects of my life that I did not make any deliberate choices in business or in my personal life. I was not building anything in either one. I was just treading water. I knew this about myself and knew it was holding me back. But I did not know how to change.

I was also in my early thirties, and I felt a great deal of pressure to have a successful romantic relationship. Even now, I am embarrassed to admit to this. My friends were getting married, even divorced. But for me, practicing yoga, running a business and living alone felt completely inadequate compared to having a relationship, successful or not. So I clung to an on-again/off-again relationship that was hardly romantic and was certainly not successful or enviable in any way. It kept me busy. It distracted me from everything I love about myself and every quality in life I enjoy. I remember saying the words to him, "You take all the fun out of me." I felt defeated daily.

I am the only one responsible for remaining in this situation so long. I was the only one responsible for my rut, the number one reason being that I was dishonest with myself. I was disconnected from myself and from everyone else in my life that really cared about me. My pride prevented me from telling anyone how unhappy I was and prevented me from asking for help. I pretended everything was okay. I made such rational excuses for him and his behavior that even *I* believed them. Every day I grew further away from my truest self.

I read somewhere that we only let people treat us as poorly as we will treat ourselves. The moment someone treats us worse than we treat ourselves, we end the relationship. I believe this. I was sick, my confidence and self-worth were shot, and that was reflected in my choice of a partner. Yet I was full of pride and feared public failure. I still wish sometimes that I had the courage to end it all before it ever took off. But timing is everything, and if it is the consequence of where I am know, I will gladly accept it.

My saving grace as the relationship unraveled was working with a mentor. I needed help running the yoga studio. I was alone in a new business experience. I had also just started a new medication, which included such daily side effects as flu symptoms, depression, and anxiety. I clearly needed help. Working with a mentor who saw my potential and raved over even my small daily successes improved my confidence and increased the clarity of my long-term vision. I lived each day more deliberately. I slowly cut away everything about my life that drained me.

When momentum increases, even the tiniest amount of momentum, the Universe steps in. Albert Einstein said: "Nothing happens until something moves." I had a heartbeat, so I started moving. I developed a vision. The vision led to a goal. I found that having a vision enabled the Universe to give me what I needed to make it materialize. New doors opened with new opportunities, and I was clear enough to see them.

During my lowest point, I also see now that part of my problem was that I stopped making my personal yoga and meditation practice a priority. And when this happened, I lost connection to myself and my own truth. When I made the choice to bring it back into the forefront of my life, I was able to make positive changes.

How do you know when you are in a groove or in a rut? You are in a rut when you stop growing. When all you encounter is your own resistance, recognize that as the sign it is time to start climbing your way out. The Universe wants a garden of blooming flowers, and when you decide to start blooming, the Universe will start providing what you will need in order to grow. When you are ready, you do not see obstacles, you do not hear "no." You discover a new path and see the opportunities instead of the dead ends. But holding on to the mediocre is clinging to a slow death. Open your hand and let it go. Something better is about to drop into your palm!

CHAPTER 5

CHOOSE A PARTNER WHO COMPLEMENTS YOUR STRENGTHS

*"You know you're in love when you can't fall asleep
because reality is finally better than your dreams."*

— DR. SEUSS

I STARTED DATING my husband in December. By March we were engaged, and in September we married. We would have married sooner, but that was the earliest his family could be in from Greece, and we wanted our families to take part in the celebrations. Most of our families and even many of my good friends were first introduced to each other at our engagement party, bridal shower and wedding reception.

People's true nature comes out during joyful times. I cannot tell you how many people said nasty things behind my back which of course made their way back to me because everything always does when people say mean things. The funny thing is that most of those people were not really *in* my life; they were on the periphery of my life. They were part of that old rut and on their way out of my life. My relationship with my husband merely stepped up the process. So many friends and acquaintances poured out their love for us too. But what I discovered was that the brightest light casts the deepest shadow.

I have heard that marriage and relationships are hard. I no longer believe that. Yes, my relationships with every man I dated before Yanni was challenging, but that's because they were not right for me. My relationship with Yanni is easy. I would say one of my greatest accomplishments and blessings is that I chose a man who makes things easy for me as my life partner.

There are many different types of relationships and marriages. My aunt, who has since passed away, was married many happy years. She lived full time in North Carolina and later Tennessee while her husband lived full time in Michigan! My aunt used to smile and say, "Twenty-five years of marriage and six weeks together!" As a younger girl this seemed crazy to me. But as I got older, I realized that love could have many faces and many manifestations, and different things are right for different people.

I do not know what is right for someone else, but I will say that if life is full of resistance then let it go. I believe it does take compromise; after all, you are two people coming together to make one life. But of all the difficult things I deal with in my life, my relationship is the easiest. I do not have to make excuses for my husband or for his behavior. I do not have to hide anything about him or about myself to our loved ones. Everything about who we are and how we interact is out in the open and carries no shame or embarrassment.

I bring this up because I have made excuses for boyfriends in my past:

"You don't know him."

"You don't see how he is with me when we are alone."

"You don't get his sense of humor."

"He had to work tonight. He can't make it."

Again, I think I believed all of these excuses because I was operating under the presumption that relationships are hard.

But when I starting dating Yanni, I never needed to excuse anything. He never stood me up for a family event or any other event I had previously committed us to. I never had to excuse his treatment of me or his behavior in public.

When I see others going through what I used to go through, I want them to know it does not have to be that way. There are other partners out there who will give us respect, see our worth, and enjoy our company. We should not have to make excuses for our life partners.

Of course Yanni and I do disagree, and we do bicker. But when it is all over, I do not even remember what it was about in the first place. We do not hold grudges. We may disagree with each other, but we are careful not to do or say something that would cause irreparable harm to the other person.

I am not here to dictate what to do, but to prescribe what works, not just in romantic relationships, but in all different kinds of relationships. As human beings, we will continue to grow as time passes, so we must choose to invite the person we are with along with us. Growth will occur either separately or together.

This is because we are either growing or dying. Nothing in life just stands still. Relationships are continually growing or gradually dying too. In my relationship with Yanni, I applied what I learned from my previous one. In order for Yanni and I to have any chance of a successful relationship, he would have to step in to work at the yoga studio because that is where I spent most of my time. Because of Yanni, the business grew in ways it never could have without him. Yanni took over the business side of the studio—negotiating with landlords and supplies, marketing, social media, and business development. And that left me free to focus on teaching, training teachers, and class development. When I travel for yoga workshops, Yanni always accompanies me because, as he says, "If you're learning and growing your knowledge, and I'm not, we'll grow apart." I married a very wise man!

Yanni and I both block out time to do our own separate things. He is an avid rock climber. I am a writer. We do not need to spend every minute of our free time together, but we do have to stay on the same frequency even when we are apart.

All relationships strengthen through growth or weaken through stagnation. You need to regularly sprinkle fertilizer–shared interests, mutual support, time together and apart—on your relationships to keep them healthy and nurtured. Otherwise, they will shrivel and die.

CHAPTER 6

LET GO OR BE DRAGGED

*"To let go is to release the images and emotions,
the grudges and fears, the clingings and
disappointments of the past that bind our spirit."*

–Jack Kornfield

TIME AND PATIENCE are required to make anything work. But so many of us, myself included, suffer the pain of getting dragged along when it is time to just let go. Eventually the pain of being dragged does overcome the perceived pain of letting go.

There is an easier way, and that is to focus more on the *what* and less on the *how*. What are our goals? What life are we creating? What does it look like? This vision is the *what* on which we need to be clear. It is okay to change our minds as we go. Sometimes we do not know exactly what we want until we get it and then we continue to improve it. But we always need to have a starting point.

The *how* is just that, tactics of how you go about creating your *what*. The *how* is basically how we spend our day living because life happens one day at time. Our day-to-day activities and routines are really important. This is why I love the Eastern Healing Arts. They help me create a structure that optimizes daily harmony.

But clinging to the *how* and losing sight of the *what* limits the possibilities of the Universe because we become so focused on the details that it allows no room for miracles beyond what our own minds can see.

So many opportunities have come into our lives in ways we could never have imagined. Understanding that tactics can be changed and habits can be both made and broken is imperative for our growth and personal empowerment.

I clung to a lousy relationship because I wanted to be in a relationship. I actually wanted to be in a loving, happy, healthy relationship that brought out the best in me, my partner, and the world. But I clung to a mess and tried to hold onto it. I was clinging to the *how*. I refused to see that other people and better relationships could be possible for me. Eventually, the pain of being dragged got too great so I let it go.

My business runs the same way. I relocated the studio after five and a half years in one location. The move was expensive, time and energy consuming. But my husband and I kept our minds on the *what*: create a beautiful studio to provide a place for transformation for ourselves and our clients that would be the best part of everyone's day. We needed a new location for this to happen. The location we were in no longer made this possible. Going through the headache and hardship of relocating and letting go of a space that no longer served the vision was easier than staying and trying to force the wrong location to be right.

Our happiness in life is in direct proportion to our ability to embrace the unknown and to grow comfortably with being uncomfortable. The road twists and turns unexpectedly. It is essential to have a clear vision and clear goals, but trust and expect that we will deviate from the plan as time goes on. The *how* continually shifts, but when connected to our goals at the core of our being and at the very level of our souls, we will be unmoved and will be able to let go.

Here are a few things I have had to let go of because they started dragging me down:

- Friendships—People grow apart.
- Lovers—Need I say anymore on this?

- Living conditions—I learned that home is wherever Yanni and I are creating our lives together, and that even if eventually I am alone again, then home is wherever I am.
- Clothes—I just cleaned out my closet. We all wear the same five items every week anyway.
- Employees—This is always extremely difficult. Training teachers entails a lot of time and effort, and I usually grow very close to them. But no one sticks around forever, and there is always someone else willing to become the next great fit if given the opportunity.
- Clients—Problematic clients are usually more trouble than they are worth.
- Money—I have had some good deals and some bad ones that have cost tens of thousands of dollars. I learned that sometimes it is best to cut my losses, let it go, and move on.
- Certain types of food—I miss tuna. I have not eaten anything with a high mercury content since the MS diagnosis.

I can go on and on with this list. You probably can too. And you know what? Life also goes on. My life has gone on, and so will yours. When you connect to your life at the soul level, everything else is just a tool for expressing your life and manifesting yourself in the world. But it is not you. Let go of anything dragging you down. It is simple but not easy to do, yet it is oh so necessary. Nourish yourself at the level of your soul.

CHAPTER 7

THE YIN AND YANG OF SAYING NO

"No is a complete sentence."

—Annie LaMott

I would never describe myself as a people pleaser, but I definitely enjoy taking part in the happiness rather than the disappointment of anyone. And really, what is so wrong with that? Who does not love seeing someone smile or bringing out someone's great joy and bright light? It is one of the things I enjoy so much about having a yoga studio: I am surrounded by happy people, and our classes get to be the best part of their day.

But sometimes people ask things of me for which I need to say no. And I do. At times I avoid it, put it off for another conversation. Sometimes it gets stuck in my mouth on the way out. But I learned to hold firm to my *no* nonetheless: I discovered that every time I said no, I was actually saying yes to something else. Every no is a choice, a step in a new direction—a deliberate step *away* from one thing and *toward* another.

As my confidence grew, so did the vision of the life I wished to create for myself. Improved personal empowerment allowed me to make clear decisions. A life is made one decision at a time. With every yes and every no, the foundation is laid and the vision begins to manifest. This is what happened for me, and this can happen for all of us.

I have discovered that what really makes people happy is our own happiness. People need to see that happiness is a possibility, and inner joy and happiness spread outward and uplift those around us. Making nourishing choices supplies abundant energy and joy to spread around. My own inner happiness shows others what is possible for them because I have demonstrated these possibilities in my own life. We love other people for the qualities they bring out within ourselves.

So bring out people's joy and possibilities through your own joy that comes with doing what is right for you. Embrace your inner voice when the *no* crops up. Because the *yes* is right there on the flip side of that coin, and your heart and soul want that *yes* to see the light.

When the vision of your life and your goals is clear, you free yourself from any guilt you associate with making choices whether the decision is yes or no. The next time your heart and your gut say no, simply ask yourself: When I say no to this, what am I really saying yes too? Saying no does not create a dead end. It offers a new beginning.

CHAPTER 8

IN THE PRESENCE OF A SAINT: AMMA

"As you perform good actions selflessly, true love will blossom, which will purify our emotional mind."

—*AMMA*

AMMA IS THE Hugging Saint of India whom I first discovered back in 2004. I read that Amma travels the world giving hugs to millions of people from every walk of life. They often stand in line, sometimes for hours, to receive their hug. It seemed Amma gave much more than an embrace. She seemed to impart hope, redemption, forgiveness, and more to her followers. Other than noting this, I really did not think any more about it.

Let's fast-forward to 2013 when I discovered that one of my students had been going to see Amma in New York City every year for her hug. That year, this student invited me along. So, on a blazing hot July day, we boarded the 5:30 a.m. bus from Scranton, PA, to Port Authority, ready to wait in line for our hugs. My student explained the process of getting this preternatural hug which involved group numbers and individual numbers and lines that shifted from the Javits Center auditorium seats to the stage on which Amma sat. It was a process, to say the least, a process that took hours.

Like many hundreds of others, my student and I showed up before the Javits Center was officially opened. But when we were allowed in, I could not believe the production I witnessed. Food carts, chai stands, clothes, healing arts, makeshift restaurants, coffee carts, jewelry, skin care, statues, herbs, and every imaginable Ayurvedic supplements were on display. It was like walking into an open market in India except that the market was indoors in New York City. All the proceeds benefitted Amma's non-profit organization for worldwide humanitarian aid. The scene was mind-blowing, but what followed actually changed my life.

I had been studying Eastern Healing Arts for a long time, and I had already experienced many inexplicable things. But what I experienced with Amma surpassed everything else. The day opened with Amma's entrance and a group meditation led by one of her closest disciples. I could have listened to this man's deep, rich-toned voice all day, and, quite frankly, I actually did since he continued to speak and chant and tell stories after the meditation. The energy in the room was powerful, and I felt the vibration in every cell of my being.

After the meditation, the group lines began to form. My friend and I chose seats fairly close to the front, so we had an excellent view of Amma. My friend explained that she enjoyed remaining in her seat watching others getting their hugs until it was her time even though she could have shopped, eaten, talked and generally enjoyed the open market.

Being new to the whole experience, I stayed with my friend and watched. I was mesmerized. I saw this small Indian woman, dressed all in white, doing the impossible. It seemed as if she was in two different places simultaneously. She hugged one person with her full attention while she blessed photos and mala beads, accepted gifts, and talked to her staff. Watching Amma, I had for the first time a true understanding of seeing a master in two places at once and connecting with people in the flesh on many planes.

In India, people believe the gods and saints walk among us. With that in mind, a revelation occurred: Amma seemed to be the Hindu goddess who is depicted with many arms because that is exactly what I saw, Amma's arms reaching and hugging and blessing, all at the same time. I did not know this at the time, but Amma is considered an incarnation of Kali, the Hindu goddess depicted with four arms and hands. Kali is considered both the mother creator and the destroyer, like Shiva who is also the lord of yoga.

I told this story a few years later while sitting in front of Amma with my same friend who introduced me to the event. We were reminiscing about our first experience, and I told her what I had seen, about all the arms and her being everywhere at once. My friend turned to me, ashen, and said, "Lara, you saw her as Kali." I did not know what she meant. She explained about the goddess and Amma's believed connection. She said she always thought it was a figure of speech, but on hearing my experience she realized that maybe she really does physically appear to people in that form. I got chills all over.

Amma has never appeared to me again in that way, but I know what I saw the first time. It was not even a fleeting image. I sat there mesmerized, not quite understanding what I was observing on one level, but knowing how special it was on another.

When I think back on it, I am reminded that there are many things in life we do not understand. But that does not make them impossible!

CHAPTER 9

THE YIN AND YANG OF GIVING AND RECEIVING

*"Should not the giver be thankful that the receiver
received? Is not giving a need? Is not receiving, mercy?"*

—*FRIEDRICH NIETZSCHE*

EVERY ONE OF us has at some time deflected a compliment or has been embarrassed when someone said something kind to us or expressed appreciation for us. I still get uncomfortable about this in regards to my business accomplishments when my husband says nice things about me to our yoga students inside the studio. He loves to let people know about every award and workshop I am invited to outside the studio. And yes, this is all great for my students to know, but it brings up deep feelings of unworthiness in me. It is a lesson, an opportunity for me to practice not batting the compliment away. Instead, during these times, I take a deep breath, smile, and say thank you..

Here is the teaching: Giving and receiving happen on the same channel. If one way is blocked, and we are unable to receive, the other way is blocked too. It is the law of Yin and Yang. Giving and receiving need each other, and we need to be able to fully embrace both.

Going to see Amma every year and getting my hug has also helped me work through feelings of unworthiness. It is hard to explain, but part of Amma's gift to the world is unconditional love. I had a student from

India years ago who grew up in the small town near where Amma grew up. She said people would line up outside Amma's house and around the block to get a hug.

I was very nervous the first time I met Amma. I did not feel worthy of this hug from a person who did not even know me. That time, those feelings of unworthiness manifested in the material world—I lost my ticket for my hug, and I knew I could not get a hug without my ticket. All through the hours of waiting, browsing the goods for sale, meditating, chanting, listening to the speaker, and watching the videos of Amma and her work, I was excited and nervous. The closer I got to my turn to get a hug, the more nervous I became. And when it was nearly time for me to present my ticket, I reached into my purse and could not find it. I was devastated, yet relieved. As much as I wanted the hug, I did not feel worthy of it.

I had to confess to my friend—who was an Amma "regular"—that I had lost my ticket. She remained reassuringly calm, had me dump out my entire purse, and we searched every inch of it. And there was the ticket!

In talking to other first timers there, I learned my story was not unusual. We carry around such feelings of unworthiness that it is scary, even palpable, to receive such unconditional love from a complete stranger. We are not used to unconditional love, so it feels uncomfortable, and we create ways to deflect it, just like we deflect compliments.

In the year that passed between my first Darshan (that is what Amma's hugs are called) and my second one, a lot had changed in my life. The studio was settled into its new location and everything about the old space and all those old relationships and patterns were purged from my life. I ramped up my meditation practice and spent the summer immersed in a personal manifestation course with a good friend. I did a lot of work on myself at the very core of my spirit.

The second time I attended Amma's Darshan I was eager to receive my hug. Over that year, I had become more comfortable with receiving in all kinds of ways. I was much better at receiving compliments, and I was also better at giving them too. My own capacity for love was greater all around—both for giving and receiving. When my turn came around, I was ready. I was ready to be that open channel of love, where love flowed freely because love does not care if we are giving or getting it. Love just is. And that is what I learned from Amma, and that is why we cannot cut someone off from giving up a beautiful compliment. Doing so cuts off the love and robs that person of the opportunity to feel and express love.

The moral here is to avoid self-sabotage; avoid cutting off the love. Condition yourself for a continuous flow of love by understanding and practicing the art of giving *and* receiving, The Yin and the Yang. Start with accepting compliments. Simply smile and say thank you. And see how happy that other person is. See the love and joy in their hearts re-flected in their eyes. By saying thank you and saying yes, you allow that person's love to shine forth and connect their love with your own inner love and joy. It is a circle of giving and receiving, a circle of love.

CHAPTER 10

THE YIN AND YANG OF SAYING YES

*"I have enjoyed life a lot more by saying
'yes' than by saying 'no.'"*

—Richard Branson

No one in my immediate family has ever participated in one of my classes, not one yoga class, not one meditation, not one workshop. And forget about my own classes or studio! They have never taken any kind of Eastern Healing Art anywhere from anyone. While I love my family, I am certainly not here to teach them about my path. I live by what is right in my own heart, and allow them to do the same.

But family being family, sometimes our paths cross, usually during the holidays. Every year when the holidays roll around and my family comes to visit, inevitably they take me out of my comfort zone.

I thrive with routine and structure. I maintain particular habits for just about every part of my life—from physical practices, to what I eat, to the bedtime I keep. Family visits, of course, throw that all out of whack.

And this is where the power of yes comes in and transforms my discomfort and annoyance with having my routines disrupted into acceptance and appreciation of my loved ones. To everything they ask of me, I just say yes.

- "Do you want to have a cup of coffee?"
  " Yes."
- "How about I make you a special dessert for tonight?"
  "Absolutely!"
- "Be ready at noon to go shopping?"
  "Sure."
- "Can we watch this certain movie right now?"
  " OK!"
- "How about the whole family meets at your place for dinner?"
  " No problem."

None of these requests are challenging in and of themselves. I make them challenging when I greet them with resistance. Saying yes drops all the resistance. My family is not asking anything horrible of me. By saying yes we are simply setting aside all of our issues, grudges and preferences. I started saying yes, and this simple action has transformed my stress around the holidays, my visits with family, and my enjoyment of time with family.

My husband, who is Greek, and I are blessed to have a wonderful family we visit every year in Greece. Of course, these visits are filled with taking in the magic of Greece and spending a lot of time with our family. Much of that time centers around food and drink. Now this might seem like a little thing, but if you have never had a Greek coffee, you cannot fully appreciate how strong it is. Combine that with hours in the unrelenting sun, and I am ready to shrivel up from dehydration and coffee-induced restlessness.

Yet, it brings my family great joy to have another cup of coffee. Each cup is made by hand over an open flame and lovingly brewed to perfection. We sit for hours and simply enjoy each other's company with no agenda, just sipping coffee. Generally, this sitting and sipping go on longer than I prefer. As I have mentioned, I am a person who is most comfortable with routines, and one of my routines is that I go to bed early. But the disappointment it would bring my family to say no to another cup of coffee far outweighs my personal preferences for my bedtime. My ultimate vision for the life I am creating is harmony in the family, and saying yes keeps the harmony, brings great joy, and makes things easier for all of us—my husband, our family, and me.

Another way I am nudged out of my comfort zone with our Greek family is when we spend the day or days shopping. I am not an avid shopper. I am not a patient shopper. I get tired, overwhelmed by stuff, and grumpy being out all day. But when I am visiting with the family or they visit me, and they want to go shopping, the answer is yes. I apply this to food too. I eat in restaurants that are not necessarily my preference, and are at times during the day that do not usually work for me, but I keep my eye on my ultimate goal, family harmony, and I just say yes.

Try it. Drop all of your resistance to your routine and give up control. Embrace the yes and be in harmony with your family. You may even get a few good family recipes and some new clothes out it!

CHAPTER 11

ANXIETY: FROM ONE TO TEN

"Nothing can bring you peace but yourself."

—*RALPH WALDO EMERSON*

LET'S TALK A little more about anxiety. Sometimes I can have all the best intentions by practicing yoga, meditating and being surrounded by wonderful people, but still sometimes there it is, showing up in my gut like a lump.

Sometimes it manifests in my stomach. This is a very common place for most of us because fear of the unknown is connected to the Earth Element in Taoism and Chinese Medicine. In yoga, the stomach or solar plexus is associated with the third chakra and personal power. It is one of the most commonly blocked chakras.

Other times I actually feel the anxiety in my blood. It is like my very body vibrates with it, and I feel it pulsing in my veins. This is because anxiety—not exactly worry which is Earth Element—is excess Fire and can show up in one's circulatory system. It is the kind of anxiety that leads to shortness of breath, accelerated heartbeat, maybe excess sweating and an all-around craziness. That kind of anxiety is, in a sense, hardwired into our system. It is a natural response from the nervous system that, as I mentioned above, I have been forced to master so it does not master me. It is also the kind that can bring on an adult *meltdown* which is the opposite of a childish meltdown. I do not cry and scream and throw myself on the floor, but instead I go inward. I feel unable to cope and show up in the way that I need to. I stay in bed. I turn off my phone. I ask Yanni or my assistant manager to handle the studio for me.

I am shining the light on this because if I had not mentioned it, no one would know this about me. I manage a successful business and a strong marriage while keeping up friendships and family relationships. Being a small business owner means that I work potentially all the time. (There is no such thing as nine to five or paid time off in small business ownership.)

Again, part of me really thrives on this, and that is why I have set up my life like this. I enjoy being challenged. I like to be busy and creative and see the fruits of my labors manifest. I like to create new programs and inspire other people. I like taking on new challenges, and I enjoy a fully scheduled day. But once out of balance, this fuel pulsing in my veins gets toxic.

Here is my trick: I have discovered that I cannot be at a ten all day long. When I am, I implode. It is too much, and my nervous system cannot handle it. I have to plan and schedule my days, weeks, and years for when I can be at a ten and when I cannot.

Let me explain. Being at a ten means I am on. I am totally in my game, maybe teaching a class, connecting with students, training the staff, and writing the business blogs. A lot of things require me to be at a ten during my day to be successful. And it is my willingness to give a ten to all of these things that has paved the way to my success and keeps me going. A lot of people desire a lot of things but are not willing to put in the time, effort, and energy required. I put it in and then some. As I said earlier, I am an all or nothing kind of girl. I do not do anything half way.

Everything that takes all of my attention, focus, and commitment is me at a ten. And I cannot sustain a ten all day long, every day, without an end in sight. I did this before during the first few years when I opened the studio, and it was slowly killing me. I had to make changes.

Now I schedule time when I let go of the ten and allow myself to be at a zero or maybe a five. Maybe a minus five! I allow it, and life goes on. The studio goes on. Classes continue. Students still show up.

We can only give what we have in abundance. Being in the Eastern Healing Arts, I give a lot of myself, and if my energy is depleted, everything begins to fail. I have to take the time I need to recharge, to fill up my tank, enabling me to give to others through my teaching, writing, and mentoring. Filling our own reservoirs will make us better at being available for others.

No one can be at a ten all day long. Most days, I have an afternoon coffee break. I speak about this a lot with the studio owners I mentor. Because of the nature of most yoga studios where classes are scheduled from early morning to late at night, I always focus a part of my mind on the studio even if I am not physically there. I used to feel a lot of guilt about not being in the studio every hour it was opened. But we are open for classes 67 hours a week. And this does not count any time for the other aspects of business ownership that fall under my command. Being there all the time became impossible. I had to let it go.

But being *absent* triggered my anxiety. What if the teacher cannot make it in? What if the desk staff does not know what to do? What if there is a problem? My mind and toxic rocket fuel raged on and on.

Then I discovered my one to ten of anxiety management. When I scheduled the time to let go, I still felt in control, yet I could recharge myself.

How I actually do this takes different forms. There are times in the day when I do not check anything on my phone because I know if I see it, I will feel the need to attend to it immediately, and that will spike my anxiety. If I am not ready to be at a ten for the studio, I meditate, take a coffee or tea break, take a nap, phone my mentor, or I go on a sabbatical in the Greek Islands with my husband. As I said, it takes many different forms, and I have it scheduled in accordingly throughout the day, week, and year.

You can do this too. A lot of responsibilities pull on you, from business to family, to personal health and more. Do not be at a ten all day long. You will burn out. Schedule in the time to recharge. You will find you are more focused and joyful in the times you are giving outwardly, and you will learn to relax inwardly.

CHAPTER 12

BEGINNING MY MEDITATION PRACTICE

"The thing about meditation is that you become more and more YOU."

—DAVID LYNCH

I TOOK MY first official meditation class in 2006. I was familiar with the concept of meditation, had certainly read a lot about it, and knew a lot in theory but not so much in practice.

I had been practicing and teaching yoga regularly for five years, but I did not have a sitting practice apart from yoga asana (posture). When a good friend asked me to take a meditation class with her, I was both curious and excited. The class was a series of lessons with just the two of us plus the teacher. This was the start of my love for meditation.

What I have learned through the actual experience of meditation is that anyone can do it. I have heard a lot of excuses over the years about why a person cannot meditate, why a person does not want to, or does not need to, or, my favorite, "It just isn't my thing." I have said most of these myself too when I have not wanted to stick to practice, when it felt uncomfortable or inconvenient.

But in my experience, *anyone* can meditate, and *everyone* can benefit from meditation. It does not take any special gift or insight or special knowledge of the chakras, prana or qi. All it takes is the will to get started.

My first commitment into consistent meditation rewarded me with despair and grief. I cried out loud and wept big juicy tears in the class. I was shocked. What was this? Where was my pure bliss and my inner peace?

But meditation shows me what I am and what I am not. I was not peaceful. I do not think I was unhappy per say, but I was uncomfortable and probably depressed. It was three years after being diagnosed with MS, and it was summer, which can be a difficult time for MS sufferers. For reasons unknown, MS patients seem to be more susceptible to the discomforts of hot, humid weather, and in Washington, D.C., summers are sweltering. Although I thrive in my hot yoga practice, it seems to be the only place where heat serves me well. So there I was, in the middle of summer, uncomfortable in my body, and resisting, resisting, resisting. I had to block out the reality of the heat just to get through my day. I was in a relationship that did not fully support me with a man who did little to encourage or empower me. My life was not nearly unfolding in the way I had planned.

Meditation smacked me into the reality of myself. It showed me exactly who I was and where I was. I was sad and exhausted. My resistance to being inside my body was wearing down my inner spirit. When I finally became still, I saw these truths right down to the very cells of my being. And I cried...and cried...and cried.

But my teacher encouraged me to stick with the practice. I had made a commitment to myself and to my friend. Therefore, I stuck with the meditation class and the home assignments which included meditating on my own. And with every breath, my resistance to myself started to dissolve, and from there the bliss of truth really did shine through.

I am no different from you. We may have different particulars to our stories, but in essence we are all the same. Meditation connects us with the parts of ourselves that stay constant throughout the ups and downs of daily life. So if you want to connect with your truth and see who you really are and come into a bigger understanding of who you could be, then meditate.

CHAPTER 13

INHALING AND EXHALING

"Blessed are they who are intimate with their Breath,
for they shall receive the 'I Can' of the Universe."

—THE BEATITUDES (AS TRANSLATED DIRECTLY
FROM THE BIBLE IN ARAMAIC)

I LOVE HAVING a yoga studio and living my Dharma because it allows for such great self- study. I continually reflect on my personal patterns, both small daily patterns and longer life phase patterns. I have learned to see the choices I make in my daily routine.

Inhaling is nourishing. It fills our lungs, brings the life force right into the body. Bringing air into the lungs is our direct exchange with the Universe, where the internal and external meet and become one. It is a life-long intercourse; we might as well make it a passionate love affair.

Every time I take a yoga class, meditate, enjoy a good cup of coffee, get a solid night's sleep, connect with my loved ones, and get alone time, I am inhaling. I have gone through life phases where most of the year is an inhale—times when I am focused on being a student rather than the teacher. Preparing for teacher trainings, workshops, conferences, and seminars that further my own education can take the better part of a year for me—one long inhale. For most of us, the college years and the bulk of our childhoods are also inhales. Times of learning, taking in information, soaking up knowledge, and filling our souls are all inhales. To inhale is to receive.

Exhaling is giving. Every class I teach or every conversation I have with a student is exhaling. Training teachers and staff, networking events, and marketing are all more examples of exhaling for me.

Both inhaling and exhaling can be equally nourishing when they occur in a circle. Remember how giving and receiving are the same channel? Well, the same can be true for inhaling and exhaling.

Teaching classes and workshops, even writing my blogs and books are exhales, but when the circle is intact, students are inhaling the knowledge. Together we nourish each other. After teaching a great class, I am all at once energized and exhausted. The two extremes meet. I am so energized that I am exhausted. I am so tired that I am wide awake.

I remember when I first opened the studio and was the only teacher—and everything else! I taught every class seven days a week. I remember one day toward the end of a class when we had two more postures to go, and I looked at my students and tears pricked the back of my eyes. I had nothing more to give. It took the rest of what I had to make it through the class. I knew I needed to make changes. I was empty. I did not understand how to find balance. Even doing what we love with no inhale becomes depleting. It took time, but I slowly began to refill my bucket.

When I was diagnosed with MS, everything suddenly became an exhale. Activities that I loved and found uplifting and recharging now drained me to the bone. Now I had to very deliberately schedule inhales for myself. I went to bed early. It was necessary to carry snack bars with me because hunger turned to exhaustion. I had to carefully gauge how many steps each adventure was costing me and spend them wisely. Walking short distances required rest. I planned where I could sit or stand and gather my energy.

I bring this up because I know a lot of people deal with chronic disease and chronic pain. Inhaling and exhaling helped me manage my health challenges and my life, by both scheduling my day and by literally remembering to focus on my breath. I got through the day one breath at a time. Each breath was one step. Every move was step by step. This helped me stay positive in my mind because instead of focusing on all the things I could not do easily any more like walking, managing stairs, seeing (I did not have vision in my right eye), or practicing yoga, I focused on how I could inhale so that I had energy to exhale and do what I loved—hot yoga.

Nothing was considered impossible; everything became categorized and prioritized. If I was going to get to yoga class, my best friend picked me up. I did not have to waste any energy, any exhaling, on driving or finding a place to park. When I got to class, I could give everything to my practice, which nourished my soul even when my body felt weak and unresponsive.

I made everything a deliberate choice, what I let go of and what I kept. I got my groceries delivered. I got a laundry service. I said no to staying out late and yes to going to bed early. I needed to be asleep by a certain time of night in order to sleep through the worst side effects of the medication that I was on. If I stayed up too late, the side effects would wake me up, keep me up, and I could not get through the next day.

As I have mentioned, I have been asymptomatic for many years now and no longer take medication. Yet, I still divide my day into inhales and exhales. I think it has helped me simplify my life, and I learned that I like a simple life. I do not want to clutter my mind, my body, or my soul with unnecessary things. I want to gather energy and give it back out again. I want an open channel for giving and receiving. I strive to balance inhaling and exhaling.

I also believe that a healthy personal relationship with our own flow of inhaling and exhaling leads to healthy relationships with others, whether with lovers, friends, family, business colleagues, and even acquaintances. Anyone constantly inhaling is needy and can drain a partner. A constant exhale is equally overwhelming. We need a balance in ourselves and a balance in our relationships. Balance does not mean we become scorekeepers, tallying up how much we gave and what we can expect to receive in return. Balance means that we each get what we need, not giving more than we take, and not taking more than we give. Sometimes we need to give more, and sometimes we need to take more. But it cannot always be one-sided. Children, obviously, need to receive from their parents. But if parents continue to give and give when their children become adults and are able to take care of themselves, the parents create an imbalance which blocks their adult children's ability to give back. The tide of life both ebbs and flows.

When my husband and I were planning our lives, I told him that I do not need a lot of *stuff* or a big house filled with *things*. Let's have a life filled with experiences instead, I said. *Things* need constant attention; *experiences* happen in the moment. Moments are inhales and exhales. Giving and Receiving. Yin and Yang.

So, begin to see and understand when are you are inhaling and when are you exhaling. Continually exhaling without inhaling leads to depletion. On the same token, continually inhaling without exhaling blocks the channel of giving and receiving. The balance of both allows you to fully blossom in your life.

CHAPTER 14

BLOOM WHERE YOU ARE PLANTED

"Be present in all things. Be thankful for all things."

—MAYA ANGELOU

I HAVE ALWAYS considered myself a loner. I crave and enjoy time alone. Large crowds overwhelm me and outside of teaching classes, which I love to do, I often prefer to sit quietly and observe.

At the same time, I love carving out my own space within a crowd. The studio is in an urban setting on a busy street. Classes are full, and a lot of people are always coming in and out and chatting. I have lived in cities my whole adult life and thrive on the energy of being surrounded by people. My dad used to call me "the city mouse" when I was in my twenties. I am simultaneously a person who loves the bustle of crowds and the silence of solitude.

This is the principle of opposites, of Yin and Yang showing up again. Amidst the crowds of the people and the energy, I can easily go within and find my inner stillness. All the external movement helps create internal stillness. I have given a lot of thought to the idea of blooming where we are planted. Can we personally bloom anywhere and everywhere, and under any conditions?

Yoga and the Eastern Arts certainly teach us that contentment comes from within and that happiness cannot be a moving target. "I'll be happy as soon as I..." Well, then when we get that or achieve that, what happens next? We are still not happy or maybe worse, we are disappointed because we discover that our expectations are unreasonable. When peace comes from within, we are unmoved by our surroundings. This logic leads me to the realization that we can bloom where we are planted.

Right from the beginning, a lot of people come into the studio with a litany of excuses. The theme is the same, with few variations: "Well I might be moving soon, so I can't really commit to anything in my life right now." With that said, it means that they have one foot out the door, and they are not present where they are or what they are doing. Simply put, they are stagnating.

Remember that we are all either growing or decaying. Nothing in nature stands still. Being non-committal is a form of decaying. Instead, we have to jump into our lives with two feet. That takes commitment and, yes, probably some courage too.

Sometimes I witness these students actually move away, but they take their same selves –their thoughts, habits, routines and resistance—wherever they go. Some believe that somehow moving or changing jobs or starting a new relationship will change them without any effort on their part. I found that wherever I am, I am there. If something did not work for me in one city, it will not work in another unless I change who I am in the new city. The Universe will not sweep in and magically intervene in our free will. But the Universe will support us when we choose to evolve for the better. Evolution is what the Universe does best, but the choice is always ours.

We all know people who are happy everywhere and anywhere. They are people who make friends wherever they go whether at a party or in the parking lot, people who always seem to have something fun on their agenda and are really living life. And often we shrug that off as if it is a special talent that is not available to us.

Truthfully though, this is a skill that was cultivated. These people are no different from us. We can do this too. They have an innate understanding that happiness comes from within, and we have to make an effort to be fully present wherever we are. Once we do, we tap into the flow of the Universe. Good things start to happen because we stop resisting!

I have informally counseled a lot of people on this over the years. Some people get it, and I watch them bloom. Others resist and slowly decay. It is always a choice.

I remember when I was in my early twenties, a friend I worked with and who was quite a bit older than I said, "Lara, don't worry. There is no one choice in your life that you can make today that is going to ruin your life. There is always an opportunity to choose another direction if the first choice doesn't work out." He further told me to go for it anyway, to seize the opportunity and take the leap and if it is not what I want, then I can decide to go in a different direction, and everything will be okay. As time passed, I have found this to be true.

I am not saying that you cannot make a choice to move—like physically pick up and move. It is okay to go for it if that is what you truly want. But whatever and wherever you are living your life, choose to bloom. It may mean a new job, a new relationship, or a new living space. It may mean a new state or a new country. Great! GO FOR IT! Do not stand still and decay. Indecision is much more expensive than making a choice— even what may be the wrong choice. That is okay too. Not everything works out. So what? It does not mean that you should not do it. Getting started puts you into the flow of the Universe and because of this, more opportunities will come your way. It is time to stop resisting and start loving your life. Decide what you want and make choices. Start saying yes. And remember that in saying no to that new possibility, you are saying yes to your decay.

CHAPTER 15

SUCCESS

"The whole secret of a successful life is to find out what is one's destiny to do, and then do it."

—HENRY FORD

HOW DO WE define success? It has certainly meant different things to me at different times in my life. Right now, success means community. I know this may seem a bit contradictory since I stated earlier that I consider myself a loner. And I do crave and cherish my alone time and need it to recharge my Soul.

Even so, with every year that goes by, the importance of building and maintaining a thriving community grows stronger and stronger within my belief system and core values, and it impacts every decision I make. I can see a direct correlation between the number of people on my team and my success. And of all of the award acceptance speeches we have ever heard in any industry, none of them ever said, "I did this all myself." It takes a village! And the greater the success, the bigger the village. If we are feeling a little stagnated in our success or even burned out, then we have to take a look at our tribe. Is anyone there in our corner rooting for us every day no matter what?

We all need a community. Through community more people bring more possibilities for growth and insight, and it is through these connections with others that we manifest positive outcomes for everyone beyond our imagination. This can mean strengthening the bonds with family, friends, co-workers, colleagues, and even with the people within our communities who make our day better—the barista, librarian, or even the regular server at our favorite restaurant. I am not saying everyone has to be a close personal friend. But being authentically present with another person, even for the smallest interaction in the form of a genuine smile and eye contact, is truly rewarding. It may be small talk in some of these instances, but by putting down the phone and being fully present, I guarantee we will feel more connected, more rooted, and happier where we are at the moment. We may even find ourselves begin to bloom where we are planted!

As the power of social media grows to keep us more connected, we actually get more and more isolated. It is now much easier to hide and disconnect from the moment we are in by retreating into iPhone and Android land. The art of conversation has almost been lost to texting.

Creating and connecting to a community or becoming part of a tribe or family is where I find the most success and fulfillment personally and professionally. After all, we all need someone to shine for. Plants turn their leaves toward the sun to catch the warmth of the rays. They need this for their photosynthesis and very survival. I believe we are the same. When we shine from within ourselves first, and when our inner light is so bright that it cannot help but shine outward onto another person, wonderful things happen.

Most of us perform better when we feel good. Being *inspired* is being *In Spirit*. It is being connected to Source, to the Light, Prana, Qi, God, your highest self, the Universe, whatever name and image with which you connect. We need someone to shine for, just like the moon needs the sun. The stars are brightest on the darkest night because without the night sky, they keep to themselves. We are no different.

This is why strong community is important for success. Therefore, find your mentor, your teacher, your lover, your partner, your best friend, your family, your pet. Connect to your understanding of God. Build your tribe. Again, it is all the same channel of giving and receiving: You shine for them, and they shine for you, and the whole world gets brighter. Everyone does better. It is a win-win for everyone!

CHAPTER 16

VISION BOARDS

"Formulate and stamp indelibly on your mind a mental picture of yourself as succeeding. Hold this picture tenaciously and never permit it to fade. Your mind will seek to develop this picture!"

—DR. NORMAN VINCENT PEALE

IN TAOIST MEDITATION, the eyes are considered the first of the Five Thieves of Meditation. Everything we see immediately either attracts us or repels us. This happens both on the grand scale and on subtle levels. Without always even registering a conscious thought, we judge yes or no to everything we see.

A way to help us manifest ourselves here in our lives is with a vision board! Success is born from constant reminders of our goals *plus* taking action each day that moves us in the right direction closer to our goals. The best reminder of our goals and desires may be visual. And anyone who has ever lost balance in a yoga posture knows that where the eyes go, the body follows. A vision board helps focus our eyes on the *yes* of our lives, while prompting the body to action.

I began my vision board process with sticky notes at my workspace and a few photos tacked onto an old bulletin board that hung above my desk. This lasted for a few years and was actually very effective. Then as part of a personal creativity and manifestation course I was taking with a friend, making a vision board was one of the weekly assignments. I took time to cut out magazine photos and words and to paste them onto a poster board. I loved my finished product, but I had two issues with it. First, I did not have a convenient place to hang it. And if I was not going to look at it, then the tool was useless. Second, it was not changeable. I wanted a vision board that could grow and expand as I did. Soon I realized that technology offered the perfect solution: Instagram!

Utilizing the power of a technological platform that is in my hands, literally, to help me focus, I have been able to plant seeds of my wildest desires and manifest many wonderful experiences: new-to-me yoga postures, travel, home furnishings, clothing. I began following accounts that posted ways I wanted to be able to move, things I wanted to own, places I wanted to visit. The result was that little by little, I was attracting each of these into my life.

Everything we create begins with an idea, a vision. We all need something to work toward. (Remember that is the *what* I spoke about earlier. The *how* takes care of itself.)

Technology keeps advancing, and our vision boards can advance too! The idea is the same, only the medium has changed. If you are on Instagram, *make* it your vision board. Surround yourself with people, places, and ideas that inspire you and embody the experiences you desire. Use it to stimulate your imagination and invite new ideas, places and people into your psyche. Take time to personally choose who is coming into your feed, and what images imprint in your mind. Recognize and use your social media as a tool for manifestation. Tame your eyes, tame this stealer of inner peace and focus with a well-crafted social media account.

CHAPTER 17

GIVE WHAT YOU *WANT* TO RECEIVE

"When we give cheerfully and accept
gratefully, everyone is blessed."

—MAYA ANGELOU

ONE OF THE most common fallacies about energy is that something outside of ourselves needs to initiate the change. We often believe we have to receive something before we can give something. Actually, the reverse is true. We should give out what we wish to receive. The world reflects back to us our thoughts and actions.

Hoarding, whether physically or energetically, leads to deprivation. When we hoard, that is, when we cling to what we have out of fear of never having it again, we never feel as if we have enough. Hoarding is *poverty* mentality, and hoarders who amass fortunes still feel as if they have nothing to give. Giving, on the other hand, is *prosperity* mentality, and regardless of circumstances, cheerful givers always seem to have bountiful lives. We all have those friends who have careers or jobs that do not necessarily pay huge salaries, but they nonetheless live big, prosperous lives: They buy homes, they travel, they drive nice cars. Goodness seems to flow to them. When we look deeper at their lives, invariably they are cheerful givers. They volunteer their time. They mentor younger people. They are always available to help out a friend in need. They feel grateful, and nothing opens the channel for receiving as efficiently as gratitude and being a cheerful giver.

When we learn to trust that giving sets receiving in motion, we reap enormous rewards. If you want to be loved, love someone, everyone. If you want respect, show respect. If you want admiration, admire someone else. If you want honesty, speak the truth. If you want kindness, be kind to everyone, even those difficult people who come into our lives and challenge us to behave as our best selves. If you want to be found interesting, show interest in others. If you want attention, pay attention to others. Put down your phone when you are sharing a meal with someone. Maintain eye contact. Give one hundred percent of your focus to the person or people with whom you spend your time. Remember, giving and receiving are the Yin and Yang of life. We cannot block one without blocking the other. We cannot have one without having the other. Give and you will receive.

CHAPTER 18

THE ETERNAL QUESTION: SIMPLICITY VS. DRAMA

"In character, in manner, in style, in all things,
the supreme excellence is simplicity."

—HENRY WADSWORTH LONGFELLOW

THE POWER OF consciousness is what makes us human and sets us apart from the other creatures here in the world. We can create. We can hold a vision in our minds and manifest it in reality. I see this as one of our greatest gifts. This gift is magical!

Many spiritual teachers profess that suffering is necessary only until it is not. I interpret this as drama versus simplicity. Everyday, I see new students enter the yoga studio for the first time because they have decided they are finished living the way they have been living. Maybe they have been in chronic pain or depressed or bored or just living with a nagging sense that something better is out there for them, and that yoga will help uncover it. I see this new commitment, this willingness to try a new way of living as turning a corner away from suffering and toward peace. They are ready to take control and start creating instead of reacting.

In order to write the next new chapter of our lives, we must be willing to let go of drama and embrace a new simplicity. The decisions in my life I am most proud of, that I would make again if I went back in time, are always the ones that simplified my situation and moved me away from dramatic relationships, encounters, and situations.

Drama takes up a lot space. It encroaches on our mental energy and our physical well-being. Simplicity leaves room—more space in our heads, more time in our lives, more love in our hearts. Drama is crowded. Simplicity always has an extra place setting at the dinner table of life for opportunity and possibility.

Drama is a time-sucking, energy-draining distraction that keeps us from realizing our dreams. Simplicity brings our dreams into sharper focus and helps us manifest our visions. Drama is sneaky. It starts by planting seeds of doubts or conflicts or resentments. Drama exaggerates and lies. Drama needs a lot of attention to keep itself alive, and drama fights viciously for its own survival. Drama takes a small inconvenience and turns it into a catastrophic problem.

Simplicity, on the other hand, gives us ease and space for new opportunities and possibilities. Simplicity urges us to let go of everything we do not want or need and keeps our lives tidy and ease-filled. Simplicity rewards for focusing on the people, places, things, and ideas that are most important, most beneficial to us. Simplicity takes the biggest challenges we face and breaks them down into tiny, manageable steps that strengthen our confidence and sense of accomplishment.

When people need drama in their lives—aside from novels and films—it generally means they are fearful of living, lack confidence, and prefer to focus on the negative. People who embrace simplicity are generally successful at what they set their sights on achieving. Drama's primary purpose is to block us from our highest goals; simplicity's goal is to prioritize our lives so that what we value most is always in our sights.

What would your life be like if you were *creating* what you wanted instead of *reacting* to what comes your way? Answer this without getting bogged down by practicalities like time or money. Start creating. Energize your imagination. Begin with a vision. Move toward your vision step by step. Put it in your Instagram feed! Give it life and energy by having it brew inside your mind.

Which would you prefer, simplicity or drama? The choice really is yours. As someone who chooses simplicity, I can tell you this: A simple life is a good life, and a good life is much more fun than one filled with drama!

CHAPTER 19

SPRING: RENEWAL

*"It is spring again. The earth is like a
child that knows poems by heart."*

—*RAINER MARIA RILKE*

ARE WE THE same all year round? Taoist philosophy teaches us that actually we have seasons just like everything else in nature. We have a time for growth, grief, recharging, and even manifesting. During certain times of the year, energy flows through the body in particular tides, and when we recognize the currents, it becomes easier to go with the flow and live in harmony.

Spring is a time of new growth and new beginnings. I have lived most of my life in the Northern and Mid-Atlantic region where all the seasons are present, and have seen the first growth of the crocuses through the snow and the cherry blossoms decorate the Tidal Basin. I have noticed when the birds returned in the spring, and I heard them waking me up on what still felt like a cold winter morning. And while I have not seen it myself, many friends and students have entered my yoga studio reporting "The bears are awake." Although Yanni and I live and work in an urban environment, our city is surrounded by woods inhabited by bears, mere miles from downtown!

So what actually happens to us in spring and how do we wake up from our own hibernation? As a natural time of renewal, when internal energy flow is balanced, spring is a time we connect to creativity and new growth. How often have we heard, "As soon as the weather breaks, I'll start that project"? It just feels like the right time for something new when spring rolls around.

In the studio, I launch a lot of new programs in the spring. I offer different workshops that involve learning something new and trying something different that is appropriate to the season. I will offer advanced classes to enhance what my regular students may already know. I tap into my own creativity that blossoms in the spring and offer programs to help my students feel the energy as well.

Personally, my husband and I take a small weekend getaway every year in early spring. I need a change of scenery during this time to sharpen my creative focus. The newness of a different location helps me see things from a different angle and gain a new perspective. I can problem solve more when I am away from my everyday routine in early spring.

While spring brings blossoms of creativity, it can also bring a bit of blossoming irritability. When we are out of balance, anger and jealousy rear their ugly heads. But in balance, we connect to our own courage, set clear boundaries, and have clear judgment for good decisions. The body's chi flow is concentrated in the liver and gallbladder at this time of year. The liver holds our boundaries, and in Taoism it also houses the Spirit. The eyes are also connected to the spring season and this Wood Element. We are probably familiar with the saying that "The eyes are the window to the Soul." This vernacular saying speaks directly to some of these concepts of the spring season. We can look right into someone's eyes and see deeply into her psyche. We can look into a person's eyes and see the beauty of her soul, or we can see a person's anger and rage smoldering. When we look into someone's eyes, we see truth.

As far as physical practice goes, in addition to the liver, the gallbladder, and the eyes, spring is connected to the small muscles, tendons, and joints of the body. It is a good time to start stretching if you have been sedentary during the winter. Picture a tree. It needs really strong roots spreading deeply in the ground in order to grow tall. Trees are also flexible. They can bend in the strongest gusts of wind without breaking. They are supple.

We can be the same. Get rooted in spring. Do this through meditation and physical practice. Movement gets the body limber and keeps the joints lubricated. Tap into your Spirit with creativity and express yourself! Learn to root down so you can spring up, strong and supple. If you are too rigid, any wind that blows through your life could break you. Find the balance between strength and suppleness, between Yin and Yang.

CHAPTER 20

SUMMER: MANIFESTATION

"And so, with the sunshine and the great bursts of leaves growing on the trees, ... I had that familiar conviction that life was beginning over again with the summer."

—*F. Scott Fitzgerald*

EACH SEASON PREPARES us for the next. In spring, the Spirit fully inhabits the body. This shows up through inspiration and creativity, with clear boundaries and strong supportive roots, as well as suppleness in both mind and body. We enter the summer season ready to manifest.

Summer is connected to the heart and small intestines and also to circulation, love, joy, and laughter. Summer season is a time of doing. We attend the summer BBQs and the family reunions. It is a natural time for parties, graduations, and weddings, all of which connect us to family and friends. So if spring is a time for new growth, then summer is a time for the blossoming and flowering of the fruits of our labors. Summer governs our tongues, facilitating dialogue and connecting with others through conversation. Out of balance, however, talking and connection can become gossip and drama!

In summer, instead of creating something new and watching it sprout, the energy is more of being in the moment, manifesting, and living fully what we nurtured throughout the spring. When emotion is in balance, we connect to love and joy. Out of balance, this energy leads to nervous tension and shock. Early summer corresponds to the

Fire Element. A good example of this is when we light a match, the flame shoots up from the matchstick and then contracts; eventually it fizzles out and leaves a smoldering ember. Every event in summer is like a flame rising up and disappearing again. Summer is a time for experiences. Physically, it also connects to the large muscles of the body. This actually makes it an easier time to train the body and lose weight than in the winter. We must be careful, though, of excess training. Too much can be taxing on already stressed cardiovascular and circulatory systems. Remember, balance is key, Yin and Yang.

At the studio, we like to offer yoga immersions and private classes during summer. People are exited to be up early, to train hard, and be fully connected to the body. This is the energy of the season coming through. The summer solstice is a time of manifestation for the body, mind, and spirit of living out loud and shining brightly like a flame or like fireworks! We should say yes to the experiences that come our way in summer and be joyful!

Late summer corresponds to the Earth Element. This is the time when the fruit is at its ripest, the time for a nurturing harvest. A vacation will recharge and fill our hearts. In balance, we connect with learning and earthly knowledge, but out of balance worry can manifest in digestive issues and trouble with the stomach and spleen. School starts up again in late summer. We catch the wave of connecting to earthly and learned knowledge. Late summer is a good time for study. This is also a time in the business when adding new programs that last over the course of several weeks, or even months, are successful.

My husband and I visit family in Greece every year. When the business does well in the winter, spring and early summer season, we reap the fruits in the later summer as we take our yoga sabbatical from teaching. We need to recharge at this time of year. Being away from the studio also provides us time for self-study, planning new programs and curriculums, plus any personal adventures we want to manifest in the upcoming year. We plan, plant, grow, and harvest in harmony with the seasons.

How can *you* plan out your year to be in harmony with the energetic seasonal changes?

CHAPTER 21

FALL: REFLECTION

*"It is only the farmer who faithfully plants seeds in
the spring, who reaps a harvest in the autumn."*

—*B. C. FORBES*

FALL CORRESPONDS TO the Metal Element. Let us look again at the tree
for a visual. The leaves change from moist and ripe to dry and brittle
before falling off and being carried away by the wind. The qualities
of fall include cutting away and reflection. It can be a time of grief,
and maybe you notice a little sadness creeping into you at this time of
year. Many elderly pass away in the fall. Fall connects to the skin, and
again that juicy suppleness of summer turns to the dryness associated with the season. It connects to the nose and to the lungs where we
hold grief. Coughs, colds, and respiratory illnesses start to settle in.

But it is not all doom and gloom! I love the fall season. I love the
reflection. The Metal Element is reflective and can show us the truth. It
is a time to make amends. We can even be sentimental in the fall. Every
fall I get almost weepy, reflecting on past choices, whether I consider
them good or bad. I reminisce about good times because memories,
even happy ones, carry with them a bit of grief over times past. But I use
the reflection as an education for moving forward and creating my life.
Fall is also a time to re-nourish our integrity, a time for taking a deep
breath and moving forward in truth and in good character.

At the studio I often teach a fall workshop, maybe a meditation or workshop focusing on breath work and pranayama. It is a season of purging, of starting to clear everything from the year that weighs us down, and through the breath—the exhaling—we can easily and efficiently clear out our emotional state. I clean out my physical living area too. I use this season to rid myself of excess emotional baggage and the stuff in my house that is just taking up space and cluttering my energy. The Qi needs to flow, and clutter blocks the way. Our physical space needs to breathe just like our bodies.

Personally I reflect on the year and my personal harvest. What did I *keep* this year? This is a great exercise you can do too. Ask yourself:

- What did I learn?
- What experiences did I have?
- How did I grow in my yoga practice?
- How are my personal finances?
- What did I accomplish this year that makes me proud?
- How are my personal relationships better?
- What professional contacts did I make?

These are just a few ideas to get you brainstorming. Autumn is the time of your personal harvest for all areas of your life: emotional, physical, spiritual, financial, business, and your personal, public, and private lives. Use honest reflection to help you make informed designs for the upcoming year.

CHAPTER 22

WINTER: TRANSFORMATION

"Let us love winter, for it is the spring of genius."

—PIETRO ARETINO

WINTER, WHICH REPRESENTS the Water Element, is the season of transformation. It is a natural time to start moving inward and rebuilding from the inside out. Winter is connected with the kidneys which house our life force energy. When the kidney qi is depleted, we may feel lethargic. We may also lack willpower and self-confidence. I tell students that we need to build the strength of our spine to have a strong backbone. I mean this both physically and metaphorically. We do not want to be spineless, or wishy-washy. We should be able to stand tall in our power, self-confident with willpower and intention. All of this points to a strong qi, and winter is the most receptive time to strengthen it.

I encourage meditation at this time. I also suggest a physical practice that encourages self-nourishment. Hot Yoga is extremely popular at this time because we literally burn our issues right out of our nervous systems (The nervous system is also connected to the winter season and Water Element).

Keep in mind that because the energy is inward, it is very common at this time to feel a need to stay in, literally, and shy away from social gatherings. While a lot of holiday events take place at this time, sometimes people feel bad that they just are not up to the crowds. Feeling a little blue during the holiday season is common. We are coming out of the fall season where the energy is sentimental, the season of the lungs and of grief. Then the season shifts into the inward winter season. While the nature of the season is inward, in society it is a very outward time with holiday celebrations and New Year's parties. Feeling conflicted with our inner selves and outer expectations can deepen some of these holiday blues and seasonal depressions.

Just knowing the energy of the season and learning how that energy affects you personally can help you navigate this time. Maybe we need to carve out more personal time and make inward reflection a priority. We are all constructed a little differently, so certain seasons affect some of us more than others and bring out our natural imbalances and tendencies.

The more we understand the rhythms of the seasons and how we personally fit into those rhythms, the easier we can create a life of harmony for ourselves. We can also notice this in our loved ones.

For example, my mother-in-law loves to entertain during the winter holidays. This is also the season of my husband's birthday. When he turned forty, she wanted to throw him a big surprise party. Well, knowing that Yanni prefers to be more inward at this time of year, I saw that this was a disaster waiting to happen. I managed to tone down a big party to an intimate gathering of six: my parents, his parents, and us. It was lovely. In talking to his mom about it, she said that growing up, he always preferred smaller gatherings. He liked to invite just one friend over, even if he could have had a big party.

If you notice you do get the "holiday blues," that is okay! There is nothing wrong with you. Take time to balance your personal alone time with your family time. Maybe smaller, more intimate gatherings are better for you at this time of year. Look at choices you can make to navigate the season with more ease. You do not have to be the life of every party. Knowing yourself and recognizing the energies of your loved ones make life infinitely much more manageable and enjoyable.

CHAPTER 23

DO YOU KNOW YOUR OWN NATURE?

*"He who knows others is wise; he who
knows himself is enlightened."*

—*LAO TZU*

TAOIST FIVE ELEMENT Theory categorizes everything and everyone in the world into one of the five elements: Wood, Fire, Earth, Metal, or Water. Learning and then beginning to understand the Five Element Theory is how I began to understand myself and where I fit into the world. I am sure we have all heard that great phrase "Don't take it personally" as if it were so easy to let things slide off our backs without eliciting an emotional response. Study of the Five Element Theory examines the questions and answers of our very nature and actually provides insight on how to take things less personally.

Recognizing patterns in our behavior is the first step in moving away from taking it personally and toward self-understanding and harmony. We must start to examine what our initial response to a situation is. Do we bring an energy of anger to the situation? If so, we may need to go through the angry energy stage until everything is okay again and we can move forward. Anger is the Wood element, and like a tree, every leaf will shake when the wind blows. Afterwards, the tree still stands. Perhaps we get rattled. To others it may look like "making mountains out of mole hills." But even a small wind rustles every leaf on the tree. We must recognize it and embrace it and know that our initial reaction may be like those leaves rattling and jostling in the wind. But after the wind settles, we will still stand tall and strong, rooted into the ground. Remember, trees provide shade and shelter. People look to us for our courage in difficult situations and our ability to take the right course of action.

For others, the initial reaction is to freak out which is a characteristic of the Fire Element. We feel our pulse quicken. Our breath gets shallow. We stand at the edge of anxiety or a panic attack. If this happens, we must understand this is our nature, and this is how we react to news. We must learn to master these feelings so they do not master us. We should not make any decisions at this time but wait for the smoke to clear and our nerves to settle. It is better to wait for the fire of our nature to cool off. This is not the best time for decision making. We do not want to leap like a flame to the next branch without thinking about the choices we are making. This behavior if left unchecked will leave us with burned down trees instead of a fruitful forest.

The Earth Element is connected to knowledge. Having all the facts in place alleviates worry. We are most comfortable when we know what to expect, and we need to examine all our options before making a commitment. With a strong Earth Elemental nature, we may take our time gathering information, but once we make that decision, we move forward with confidence. This nature brings a solid, calm and grounded energy to decision making.

If any of this sounds a little ridiculous, it may be the Metal Element cutting through. Are our words sharp and cutting? Do others describe us as someone who "tells it how it is?" Are the facts more important than the fluff? And once we clearly see what we need, there are no regrets about the decision we have made. A strong Metal personality tends not to hold a grudge. We can be great in adversity, clearly seeing the issues and able to make choices that are good for the whole community without getting stuck on emotional attachments. A balanced Metal Element equals strong integrity. We may also enjoy cutting away the clutter. When something is over, it is over, and that is okay. There is no need to cling but to just move on.

For some of us the Water Element is more our style. We are comfortable going with the flow and do not need to be the chief decision maker. We may react with some insecurity or with a little depression or even internalize our feelings and preferences. How balanced we are in our element can vary the reactions. Strong confidence shows a balanced Water Element, but hypochondria and low self-esteem can flag some depletion. We may lean heavily on others, or maybe we are the shelter, providing the open arms in times of need. Both of these reactions are the tendency of a strong Water Elemental constitution.

No elemental nature is better or worse than the others. In and of themselves, they are neither good nor bad. It is all about recognizing who we are and making responsible choices from self-acceptance.

Let me share an example from my own experience. Yanni and I love to travel. His style is very watery; he likes to arrive and see what unfolds. He does not feel the need to make any plans or commitments ahead of time. I have learned to relax and accept this over the years, and it has made me a less anxious traveler when I am by his side. My tendency is to plan. I like to book ahead and know what to expect. A more earthy approach comes from me. Knowing our own and each other's nature helps us avoid miscommunication and helps us work together in a way that meets both of our needs and creates amazing travel experiences. I make the set travel plans, like booking the plane tickets. I look at the different options and cross-reference them with the studio schedule and with the family expectations. I do a little research to see what the best option is. Yanni happily packs a bag the night before, hops on the plane, and departs ready for the adventure. He is happy booking a hotel in the airport or even asking for a recommendation once we land. The first time we traveled together was almost unbearable for me, and my anxiety skyrocketed. But now that I know his nature and my own, we work together and in harmony.

The key here is that neither of us is trying to change ourselves or the other person. We simply recognize where our strengths lie versus what rattles us. We maximize the strengths and mitigate the rest. This is very simple with the right tools. Study of the Five Element Theory helps us see who we are and know our natural first reaction to a situation. It provides insight on what serves or hurts us.

Here is another example. I know sometimes I am all about my Metal Element: sharp and cutting with no nonsense. In and of itself, this is neither good nor bad, as long as I am the master of this tendency. For example, it is part of what makes me a good teacher. I have an ability to use my words and get a message to my class and students within a certain amount of time very clearly. I am good in a crisis situation because I can cut away the drama and be sharply focused.

But sometimes I can be too serious. My tongue can be too cutting. I need to recognize when and how to be softer so I do not unknowingly and needlessly hurt someone's feelings.

Harmony in life is all about knowing who we are and how we show up in a situation. The Five Element Theory also helps us recognize other people's natural tendencies so you do not take things so personally. You know your best friend is going to bring along the drama to your lunch date. It is just her way. You know your boss is going to be angry when she sees the report but then will listen to new ways to bring growth to the company and solve the problem. Stop stressing about that visit from Mom. She goes with the flow and is happy anywhere. Does your partner worry about every little thing? Give him facts and be sure to keep him in the loop.

You have many tools at your disposal to help you alleviate the stress and difficulties of daily interactions when you know your nature!

CHAPTER 24

WHAT PHASE OF LIFE ARE YOU IN?

"The bad news is time flies. The good news is you're the pilot."

—MICHAEL ALTHSULER

THE PHASES OF life are part of my favorite thing about the Five Element Theory. Let me explain this through the lens of my own life.

The first phase is the Wood phase, from the age of birth to eight years. Like springtime, our lives share the same characteristics of the season, new growth and discovery.

The Fire phase begins at age eight through thirty-two years. As I mentioned earlier, the movement of the energy is spreading like lighting a match and seeing the flame ignite upward and outward. Fire energy is hot and intense. In my Fire phase I tried a lot of different things and made new discoveries and choices. Typically the Fire phase is a very exciting time. Life is filled with heat and passion, and we possess a ton of energy and excitement for trying new things.

And like a flame that flickers and rages, the high times are very high and low times can be very low. This shows up in personal relationships. I remember being twenty years old and absolutely, positively sure my life was over when my boyfriend broke up with me. Yet somehow, here I am!

The transition from the Fire phase of life to the Earth phase is age thirty-three. A lot of people go through big life changes at this transition time. These transitions may occur a couple of years earlier or a few years later, but we will notice that between the ages of thirty-two and thirty-five we probably made or will make choices that moved us into a whole new phase of our lives: marriage or new relationship, divorce or break-up, new baby, new job, recovery from addiction, a move or a new city, going back to school or completing a degree.

I remember feeling restless when I hit my late twenties. I was not exactly sure what I wanted in my life, but I did know I wanted to create something more lasting than the existence I had. Within the next several years, I moved to a new city, opened a business, and ended a major relationship. This all occurred at my transition into the Earth phase.

And it was all perfectly timed. The Earth phase is a time for doing the work, for putting down roots. If we try everything on during the Fire phase, the Earth phase is when we decide what to wear to the party and who will accompany us. There is no need to dance with everyone. We are more settled and ready to live our lives by making some lasting changes and choices.

Before getting married, my husband and I knew we were both in the Earth phase of our lives. We finished trying things out. We were ready to build a life in one place, set down our roots, and see what we could create together.

In the Earth phase we follow through. I still like to travel and try new things because now I know who I am and what I am creating. A steady Earth phase is what allows me to enjoy many great opportunities stress free. I can leave town because I have a home to come back to. I can take a sabbatical each summer because I have a strong business and a great staff to support the studio. A clear vision of what I want keeps me motivated through the tough times. Knowing the next phase that lies ahead also keeps me going. What we do in the Earth phase greatly affects the next phase of our lives, the Metal phase.

Age fifty-eight ushers in the Metal time of life. As I mentioned previously, the Metal phase is harvest time. What the Earth phase builds, the

Metal phase reaps. Relationships, family, property, business, schooling, knowledge, financial security or insecurity at this stage depend on what we build in the Earth phase.

Good health at this phase can also be a reflection of how we treated our bodies in the previous phase. During the Fire phase, we recover easier from intense training and from injuries, but with every passing year, the consequences of our behavior—and I do not just mean in our health—are more difficult to overcome later in life.

I am not yet into my Metal phase, but I have seen emotional regret, heath issues, financial instability, and stress all manifest more deeply in this phase for individuals who did not take time to build, to dig in, and to do their work during the Earth phase. It is never too late to make peace or start caring more for our personal health, but the earlier you do it the better!

The final phase is the Water phase, which comes in at age eighty-three. This is the phase many do not reach. It is the phase of transformation and when we give it all back. We give our knowledge, wisdom, love, even our material goods and finances back. I remember when some of my older family members were downsizing their living situations in this phase. Some invited the family over to their homes and asked us what we wanted. It was ours! They did not need those things anymore and wished for us to enjoy them. Others put together boxes of items which different family members might like. Sometimes the distribution happened after death through a will.

But again, we are not just talking of material things here. The grand matriarchs and patriarchs of the family have many stories to tell. They remember the old family picnics; they can name the people in the old photos. They have wisdom to share from a long life, from hard times and good times.

The more we embrace each phase for the energy it offers us, the stronger the next phase will be. When the Fire phase is strong and exciting, filled with new experiences, we are ready and excited for the Earth phase. We do not carry feelings of loss or regret into the next phase with us. I traveled the country and lived out of a suitcase in my Fire phase when I was on tour for a year as an actor and recent college grad. I had plenty of energy, no money, and a great time. I did not have any responsibilities that required substantial amounts of money. I was not in the right phase for house payments or car payments. It was a time for exploration and new experiences, all of which I had plenty. But I would not have wanted that phase to last forever.

Now that I have more financial and personal responsibilities, I am glad of all the things I did when I had the opportunity. When my Earth phase rolled around, I welcomed it. I was happy for a solid intimate relationship. I enjoyed owning a business that I could expand and in a career that I loved rather than merely having a job to pay the bills. I look around every day at our beautiful home and sometimes I even say out loud, "I'm so happy we live here and don't have to think about moving any time soon." Every choice carries a different feeling with it now. In my Fire phase I had several different jobs that paid the bills, and I lived in many different dwellings. My Earth phase brought a desire for something more stable, plus a willingness to put in the time, effort, and energy for the rewards.

I notice that most people go awry at this last part I mentioned, that is the "willingness to put in the time, effort, and energy for the rewards." I see this often, both inside and outside of the yoga room. A lot of students want the results of practice: a quiet mind, less stress, more flexibility, less pain, a supple spine. But they are not willing to put in the time and the effort this demands. This requires stepping up to the challenges of the Earth phase. We do not get to our harvest without the work. There are no shortcuts. We must put in the time to reap the rewards. People want to skip from the exciting Wood phase, where everything is new and the Fire phase where everything is full of passion and excitement, right to the Metal phase of enjoying the bounty. But it just does not work like that. Giving and receiving are the same channel. We cannot take without giving first. There is nothing to enjoy without doing our part.

I hope you can start to see these different phases and how they are reflected in your own life. Seeing the patterns of energy helps you make good decisions and maximize your choices and your life!

And if you feel behind, do not worry about anything you did not do. The time is now. Start now, here, today, with what you have and where you are. Waste no energy on what you might have done if you had known. Now you know! You are not too late. You are right on time. The Universe is one hundred percent behind you.

CHAPTER 25

THE ART OF AGING

*"Aging is not lost youth, but a new stage
of opportunity and strength."*

–Betty Friedan

I REMEMBER SITTING over a table after class with one of my students. I was fixated on a recent breakup I had experienced and was telling him that at twenty-seven years of age, I already felt ancient. I felt as if so much of my life had already happened, and future choices were closed off to me.

My student was older, and I realize now, wiser. He laughed and said, "Lara, You are only twenty-seven. I guarantee you that in a few years, you are going to look back on your life and say 'Wow, remember when I was only twenty-seven!'" He was right.

A few years ago, I was at a family party. My great Aunt Ida was there, and we sat together. She was about ninety years old at this time. She leaned into me, took my arm and said, "Hey, Doll, want to see a picture of me when I was younger?" She then reached into her big purse and pulled out a plastic baggie with *real* photos in it. She pulled out one of these, held it up and said, "This is me at my fiftieth birthday party! Look how young I was!"

I think back often on these two conversations, especially as I approach the close of my own fortieth year. I love knowing everything that I have learned and where I am right now and would not want to go back to my younger days.

When I turned thirty, a girlfriend, who was three years older than I, told me that no one will ever say to me again, "Wow, you accomplished that at such a young age!" She said that no one thinks that after thirty is young anymore.

I opened Steamtown Yoga later that same year, feeling completely inexperienced and unprepared. Even though in the context of relationships I felt old, in my business I felt so young. It seemed as if everyone, including the students, was older than I was. I think this held me back in being a good leader during those first couple of years that I was in business. In 2009 I started working with my mentor, and that is really when I was able to start coming into my power.

Oddly enough, I distinctly recall when I started *feeling* like an adult. I was thirty-six. I am guessing that many had that same experience. By my mid-thirties, I felt more myself and much more confident. It was like turning a corner and everything was different, though I was still on the same street.

As I look back on my life now, I realize that life just keeps getting better and better. It does not mean life gets easier, or that nothing bad ever happens. What it means is that I become more authentically *me*. I can more easily let go of bad habits that hurt me, and I can let go of people who make my life more difficult. I am less influenced by outside opinions and more connected to my sense of purpose. This is what being an adult means to me—being true to myself while adding value to others and to the world.

No matter what age you are, live a life that is enriching, rewarding, and adds value to you and to everyone around you. You never outgrow the need for self-reflection. Taoist Philosophy teaches us to live, live, live until we die, instead of dying slowly for a long time and never really living. For me, living means setting goals and then exceeding them. What does it mean to you?

CHAPTER 26

FROM TORMENTOR TO MENTOR

"The mind is not a vessel to be filled,
but a fire to be kindled."

— *PLUTARCH*

WHEN I STARTED teaching in 2003, I felt right away that it was my life's work. I did not know I would have my own studio one day, or what different styles of yoga I would expand into throughout the years, but I am certain that I am an excellent teacher. I know I am terrible at so many things, but teaching, inspiring, and empowering others is not one of them!

The only thing I appreciate as much as teaching a great lesson is taking a great class with an awesome teacher. And when I connect with someone, one isolated class is not enough. I want that connection to deepen and strengthen. It is one of the reasons my husband and I had a whirlwind romance and marriage—because I do not do anything half way. I am all in or all out.

I met my mentor in 2009. It was an utter leap of faith. He was teaching a two-day workshop in Phoenix, and I was living in Northeastern Pennsylvania. I had my yoga studio where I taught every class. I had no discretionary travel funds. All I had was this *feeling* that working with this particular mentor was important for me. I booked the June workshop in April, which gave me two months to figure out how to pay for the workshop and flights, if I would close the studio, and if not, who would fill in for me. Then June finally arrived! After much anguish and financial wrangling, off I went, flying standby to save money.

I made it as far as Austin, Texas, before everything began to fall apart. All flights in Austin were grounded due to the weather. I was definitely going to miss the first day of the workshop and, possibly, the second day too. I was beside myself. I called my mentor's studio and asked his assistant what I should do. After leaving me on hold and consulting with my mentor, she got back on the phone and said, "Just come."

Still, I had a whole day and night in the Austin airport before I could board a plane to Phoenix. Fortunately, I met a woman, Eleda, at the airport who befriended me. Eleda's car was parked at the airport so she suggested we get out, find a hotel, and enjoy the night. The next morning we came back early to see if we could get a flight, and we did. I arrived for the second day of the workshop, and the relationship I forged with my mentor and the knowledge I gained through that one day changed the course of my business and my life. Since that time I continue to take every class, course, workshop, and one-on-one mentoring that I can. I have grown immensely during the last decade because of this consistent guidance and nurturing.

Such is a disciple/mentor relationship, a student/teacher relationship. We need someone outside ourselves to help us see, develop, and manifest our greatest qualities. Choosing a mentor can be a rigorous journey. I have friends who literally traveled throughout India in search of a mentor. For me the choice was easy—my mentor was at that time the only person doing what I needed mentoring in, specifically on how to build and sustain a successful yoga studio.

Everywhere we may notice sayings and mantras like, "I am enough," and, "You already are everything you need." I do not exactly disagree with those statements, but I could not see my own *enoughness* until I had a mentor look at me, see my potential and, most importantly, understand how to help me bring it forth into the world. I believe we are enough just as we are, but perhaps we are even better with the right support.

Nothing exists alone in a vacuum. We would never know the beauty of a full moon without the sun there to reflect it for us. And the sunset does not know its own beauty without the clouds there to show off the brilliant colors. We are the same. We need mentors and teachers in our lives to reflect our best selves.

Sometimes mentors do come in the form of tormentors. It may have been the impossible student, the difficult staff member, the rude stranger, and even the dysfunctional family member who has forced me to grow the most. Not surprisingly, it was my mentor who pointed this out to me! When things do not go smoothly, or work out as planned, or meet my desires, his answer is always "This person or situation is just forcing you to grow."

I grew. And I choose to continue to grow because we are all always either growing or dying. And death comes to us all anyway. We may as well continue our growth while we still have the choice.

When you find a teacher you connect with, go for it. We all need someone to shine for, much like the necessary polarity of Yin and Yang or the witness and the observer in yoga philosophy. They only exist because the other exists. Seek out mentors. Ask the Universe for teachers to appear. Create the space and embrace them when they arrive. You deserve it, and the world deserves to have your very best.

CHAPTER 27

WHAT DO YOU GET WHEN YOU'RE SQUEEZED?

"What do you get when you squeeze an orange? Whatever's inside the orange."

—MASTER JASON CAMPBELL

WHAT I APPRECIATE most about my study and practice of yoga and the Eastern Healing Arts is the self-knowledge. The Chinese Taoists have a saying, which translates into "Turn the Light Around." It encourages a self-illumination and a look inward for answers.

Now I certainly do not have all the answers, but I can get to know myself, my own behavior, and how I react to situations. I can use that self-knowledge to help guide me toward a better life in harmony with the Universe. After all, it makes no sense to fight against the Universe; the Universe always wins. Recognizing our own patterns of behavior is really the first step toward a life of harmony, ease, and abundance.

For example, I am prone to anxiety, what I would even call terrible and debilitating anxiety. I bring it up because I manage it so well that only people who know me really well can see it. I did not see this about myself until I was diagnosed with MS just before my twenty-sixth birthday. At that time, anxiety manifested as insomnia and tears. I cried all the time about everything and nothing. Chronic autoimmune disease can do that. Tears became the go-to stress relief, and fear of the unknown brought on the insomnia. This phase of anxiety did not last forever. Once my initial symptoms were under control and the medications into more of a routine, the anxiety dissipated.

When I opened the studio in 2007, the anxiety returned with a vengeance. But I have been able to transform it, and that transformation is worth sharing here. First of all, we need to ask ourselves the right question: What do we get when we're squeezed? And the answer is whatever is inside.

We all have our own ways to react to stress, conflict, difficulty, pain, confrontation, and roadblocks. The key is that we do not know what that reaction is until it happens. I would never have thought I had anxiety. (Honestly, I never heard that word used to describe a person's condition until I was in my thirties. In my late twenties, I did not give it a name. I simply called it, "I cry all the time.")

But when I opened the studio with no money, no local friends, no local family, no support, no students or business knowledge, I was definitely squeezed. And my insides poured out ripe with anxiety.

Fortunately, I was able to turn my anxiety into my greatest asset—anxiety became my fuel. And the most toxic substances can become the strongest sources of energy when used correctly. The radioactive element Uranium fuels nuclear submarines and weapons. Toxic Plutonium is powerful enough to launch rockets into space. My anxiety became my personal rocket fuel to launch my business to success and create whatever life I could envision for myself.

A weakness is only a weakness when it masters us instead of us mastering it. Are we stubborn or determined? Well, that depends. When we master our will, we are determined. When our will masters us, we are stubborn.

As soon as I saw this, instead of being debilitated by anxiety, I became empowered. Now when I am squeezed, awesomeness pours out with such qualities as focus, a strong work ethic, determination, and grit. My fear of failure transforms into my will to succeed. And moving toward something great is much more motivating and inspiring to me than moving away from something painful.

Sometimes we need a reason to gather our energy. Something needs to create a shift in us which is strong enough to get us moving. Anxiety does that for me. Without it, I get bored, even a little depressed. When I feel the anxiety creep in, it is time to move, time for transformation, time to launch my greatest desires to the moon and back again!

And as always, if I can do this, so can you. Be your own Master Teacher and gather the support you need.

CHAPTER 28

IN THE PRESENCE OF MASTERS

*"Find the teacher who speaks to you in
the language of your heart!"*

—*Paramahansa Yogananda*

NOTHING COMPARES TO actual in-person face time with a Master Teacher. I feel a responsibility as the owner at Steamtown Yoga and as someone who has dedicated my life to yoga practice and teaching to meet as many masters as I possibly can. When I lived in D.C., one of my Bikram students was also an Iyengar Yoga instructor. She was preparing to spend five weeks studying with BKS Iyengar, who is one of the most widely respected yoga masters, at his Southern India ashram. She said the biggest challenge was getting her affairs in order because she would be away from her *regular* life for so long. She made this rigorous travel a priority knowing Mr. Iyengar, who was already quite elderly at the time, would not live forever, and the opportunity to study directly with him was limited.

About a year after this, Mr. Iyengar came to D.C. to lecture. The event sold out before I bought my ticket. It was his last public tour, and he passed on in his mid-90s in 2014. When I think about this, I still feel a sense of loss not just because of his passing, but also for missing the chance to see a great master yogi. Now whenever I learn of an opportunity to attend any direct teaching from a master, I jump at that opportunity. Some of my favorites include His Holiness the Dalai Lama, Amma, Eckhart Tolle, Bikram Choudhury, and Deepak Chopra.

Deepak Chopra is, of course, a thought leader for positive thinking, visualization, creating health and prosperity, and yoga. I have been following Dr. Chopra's lectures, reading his books, and listening to his meditations and audio lessons for many years. I cannot even remember anymore how I first heard of his teachings. I know it was after I started my yoga practice but before I attended my first yoga teacher training with Bikram in 2003. Dr. Chopra has many impressive credentials, but I see him as a man who bridges the gap between Eastern Healing Arts and philosophy and Western medicine and philosophy. He teaches yogic principles as scientific, which is how they are taught in India. He offers a holistic view of health and life that addresses mind, body, and spirit.

Dr. Chopra is both a spiritual teacher and a United States-educated doctor. One reason I am drawn to Dr. Chopra is because my father is a physician and my mother has a PhD in Science. I grew up in a scientific household where the cause and effect concept was used to determine the consequences for my actions. Feelings and intuition were not valued as much as facts. As a family, we did not engage in a formal religious practice. So ideas about the cosmos and where I fit into this Universe came from my own experiences. Finding Deepak Chopra was a natural fit for me once I began my yoga practice. He helped me personally bridge the gap between East and West in my own life, in my thoughts, and in my family dynamics.

In 2017, I attended a program presented by Dr. Chopra and experienced the excitement of meeting a master in person. He discussed his book *You Are The Universe* which, to simplify dramatically, suggests that the entire Universe and our reality exists because of *us.* Our ideas and experiences quite literally shape and create the entire Universe. Essentially, Dr. Chopra says that the Universe is reacting to us, and knowing that consciously can help us create the reality we want.

Dr. Chopra claims yoga helps us experience our connection to the Universe and our participation in its creation. Science is closer to explaining and proving mathematically what yoga intuitively offers us as the truth, yet there remain many ideas and equations of how the physical world behaves that science and mathematical formulas still cannot explain.

With lofty ideas—such as what came first, consciousness or the Universe—expounded on by Dr. Chopra and other great minds, my personal goal was to simplify the concept into something I can digest and apply to my own daily life then teach to my students to help them improve their lives. The question I asked myself after attending the lecture was this: What reality would I create if anything was possible and if I were not confined by what I already believe to be true?

Many ideas in science once hailed as truth have been disproved and replaced with new truths. Even genetics, which until very recently maintained that our genes are set in stone and nothing can be done to change them, has been proven untrue. Genes can change! *Anything* can change.

How can we apply this knowledge to our own lives? What truths, once replaced, would change how we see ourselves and how we create our lives? Dr. Chopra talked about the Universe being made of possibilities. And those possibilities live within us, and those possibilities are endless.

I was filled with joy at the end of the evening with Dr. Chopra. Participating in a night with him showed me how many ideas that yoga addresses, once considered "out there," have become mainstream. This feels so good to me; Dr. Chopra reignited my excitement for teachings that I take for granted, teachings that I need to bring forth with greater emphasis. Since my face time with Dr. Chopra I have had great conversations about his teachings with my students, which draws me closer to them and deeper into my own teaching.

My students are often eager to hear about my experiences, my new trainings, and my ever-evolving acquisition of knowledge. They want to share their own lessons that they learned from books, meditations, and other teachers too. We all feel fortunate that publications, electronic media, and the Internet make it extremely easy for us to access information from great minds everywhere. I see it as such a positive movement for the human collective consciousness, and I am honored to play my own part in it as a teacher and owner of a yoga studio and as a student attending an event with a master such as Deepak Chopra.

One thing I always keep in mind is that while mass media have made it simple for us to connect with teachers, lessons, and ideas, nothing compares to one-on-time and being in the physical presence of a true master. Breathing the same air matters. Feeling the vibrations of the speech, and even sharing laughter matter. Our spirit and our skin absorb the experience. All of our senses participate.

I also love seeing masters because historically, Yoga, Qigong, Martial Arts, Eastern Meditations, Mantras, Mudras, and lessons are passed on from one master or Guru to one disciple. This is the traditional Eastern way of guiding. The idea of group lessons is a fairly new, Western idea. I love our Western ways. They work! I love teaching full classes at the studio which enables me to support myself through teaching—I would not be able to survive by teaching private sessions. Group classes also make the teachings accessible to many more people. Imagine if we all had to spend several months a year in India to study with a master. There would not be a lot of people studying, and the knowledge might even die out eventually. I believe it is imperative to pass the lessons on and help the whole world gain from them.

When I get the opportunity to be the student, it is easier in a practical sense to take a class than to schedule one-on-one learning. Today, not all masters are interested in taking on private students, apprentices, or disciples. But I have been fortunate to have been able to spend a few years of my own personal education with private training from my own Master Teachers, Jason Campbell and Michael Leone, and these times have been the most fruitful. Their training was in week-long segments throughout the year, some lasting up to about a month a year for several years. Master Leone opened his home to me, and I shadowed him every hour of the day. Sometimes the lessons were specific for me, and sometimes I just tagged along with whatever he had to do and whatever he was teaching at the time or developing in his own personal practice. I credit this attention and focus as one of my great strengths as a teacher. I am immersed in a lineage. I have both traditional Eastern training, coupled with practical Western studies.

And, although I am a rarity today, my time was quite limited in comparison to many others. Master Leone lived with his teacher for four years! My student who is the Iyengar teacher spent five weeks with BKS Iyengar. Ashtanga yoga practitioners often spent up to six months with Guruji, Sri K. Pattabhi Jois, returning to his ashram in Mysore, India, annually.

Master Teachers are those special individuals who can deliver the message you most need to hear in a way that you can accept. Some Master Teachers—His Holiness the Dalai Lama, Pope Francis, Mother Teresa, Amma, Thich Nhat Hanh, for example—are individuals who clearly have transcended many human weaknesses. Other Master Teachers are still as fallible as any other humans, but they are still masters at what they know and teach. One such master is Bikram Choudhury.

I spent nine weeks with Bikram, not living in his home and not one-on-one, but on a mat by his feet for fifteen hours a day. This kind of learning required leaving my regular life behind and devoting my time entirely to study. This kind of learning is not for everyone, but I know the absorption of lessons I received is unparalleled.

Today the name Bikram is surrounded by scandal and controversy, which obscures the fact very few people now acknowledge: Bikram was the master responsible for bringing yoga to the West. Virtually everyone in the United States who began practicing yoga after 1970 owes her practice to Bikram.

Before Bikram began offering his massive teacher trainings—259 people graduated with me in the fall of 2003—anyone who wanted to deeply study yoga postures and philosophy travelled to India, solo, to seek a Guru and become a yoga teacher. These teachings were given by men who had been raised practicing yoga their entire lives. The postures were impossible for most Westerners who had never moved their bodies in such extreme ways. Bikram and his Guru developed a series that anyone could practice. And then Bikram brought those postures and other yogic lessons to the West in a form accessible to the masses.

When I began my practice, I was not looking to bend my body like a contortionist. I was not looking for enlightenment. I just wanted to feel better. Bikram provided classes that did not scare me away with extreme postures, chants I did not understand, or concepts I was not ready to digest. Bikram's Beginner Yoga series met me right where I was, uncomfortable in my physical form, looking for a better way. He provided a vehicle for change. He claimed that doing his series every day for sixty days would change anyone's life. For me, he was right. After I completed my personal Sixty-Day Challenge (one ninety-minute class a day for sixty days straight) I signed up for his teacher training without hesitation.

Even though I had recently been diagnosed with MS, and I was sick from the medication, I knew I had to train with Bikram. I was scared! The training took place across the country, far away from my family, friends, doctors, and support system. But I *knew* intuitively that I had to go and train with Bikram and become a certified hot yoga teacher.

For me, studying with Bikram, just as he promised, was life changing. Merely watching Bikram work was a revelation. I had never seen anyone work the human body like Bikram did. During posture clinics, he asked the person with the worst posture to volunteer to step forward. "Who has the worst floor bow?" he asked. Inevitably someone shyly stepped up, and Bikram transformed this person's posture before our eyes.

My training took place in 2003, before smart phones, before social media, before digital cameras made taking photos a snap. No one was taking pictures of postures. Outside of the D.C. yoga studio I attended, I had never seen another person's posture before I attended training. Now, because of Instagram, Facebook, Snapchat, Twitter, blogs and websites, yoga is everywhere. We see people bending, breathing, chanting, and meditating across all media, all day long. But this was inconceivable in 2003. Back then, I saw one view of myself in a pose, and only when I was in front of the room by the mirror. Seeing another body execute a posture during training was totally new. I was astounded. Watching Bikram know exactly what to do and say to transform that body before my eyes was mesmerizing. He was a Master Teacher, and his words have proven true for me and for countless others: "Give me thirty days, I'll change your body. Give me sixty days, I'll change your life."

I watch my students transform before my eyes now. For many of my students, I am the Master Teacher. Others move on to masters who can offer them training that I cannot. As another example, one of my dear students, who started her yoga practice with me years ago, took our teacher training and eventually became our studio manager. After several years, she then moved to California specifically to work with a teacher who could provide the private instruction she craved in order to maximize her body's yogic potential. She trains privately with this teacher many hours each day and travels with her throughout the world to attend workshops as her assistant. Her practice has grown dramatically during this time, far more than it could have grown without this intense training and commitment on both her part and that of her teacher. Every aspiring master needs a master to guide the way.

For my students, I strive to connect with each of them individually. That one-on-one direct transmission makes a difference. Not everyone wants to make her whole life about yoga, but everyone wants a happier and healthier life. Not all students can live with their teachers, and not all teachers want students living with them! But the master/student relationship must be created in whatever way possible.

And this brings us back, once again, to our main theme here and in life: Yin and Yang. Nothing exists in a vacuum. No one is a master unless he has a student; and no one can be a student without a teacher. One cannot exist without the other. The master/student relationship, however it may be formed and expressed, whether through one-on-one or group classes, needs both. Without both, the lessons are lost, and no one benefits.

Remember, time with Master Teachers is limited. When the opportunity presents itself to study with a master, take it. When you are presented with the opportunity to act as a master for another, take it. Receive and give. Learn and teach. Yin and Yang.

If the universe is made of possibilities as Dr. Chopra suggests, then what would you create? Do not get hung up on how small or grand, how possible or impossible it may seem. Do not even worry if it is labor intensive or costs a lot of money. Start with the idea. Use your imagination and create a clear vision of what you want. That is where the creation begins. Have fun with this. You are full of possibilities. It is time to bring them into the light and into the world!

CHAPTER 29

PLEASE KNOCK BEFORE ENTERING: A BRIEF LESSON ON RESISTANCE

"Most of us have two lives: the life we live, and the unlived life within us. Between the two stands Resistance."

—STEVEN PRESSFIELD

RESISTANCE WEARS SO many different masks that at times it is hard to recognize. Everyone experiences resistance to some extent, but most of us fail to realize that resistance, not destruction, is the opposite of creation. Unlike destruction, which can make way for new beginnings and fresh starts, resistance stops all motion and stifles all creative output. Sometimes we confuse resistance with challenge, but challenges often bring out our greatest strengths and move us forward, forcing us to grow. Resistance, on the other hand, chokes the flow of the Universe and impedes new growth. Resistance is neither an inhale nor an exhale, but a holding of the breath instead. In defiance of nature, which is always moving and changing and evolving, resistance chooses to stand still. Resistance leads to loss of breath and eventually to decay.

I teach my students that the body responds to breath, specifically to exhales. Inhaling helps us to prepare, gather our energy and our knowledge. Exhaling helps us to make the move, find the stretch, deepen the pose, or take a step forward. Inhale is intention and exhale is action.

Progress and growth are borne from inhaling and exhaling, which create openness and compassion. This openness and compassion create space for possibility. Resistance is like a closed fist that suffocates all the options and possibilities or tries to break down the metaphoric doors to achieve its purpose. Neither of these extremes works. Resistance is not a fearful friend that needs to be soothed into movement; resistance is the unreasonable enemy that must be thrust from our lives.

How often have we wasted energy trying to break down a door to reach the next step, opportunity, posture, achievement, or relationship? We are the architects of our bodies, minds, and Souls. We built that door ourselves, choice by choice, yes by yes, and no by no. Why force our way through our own creations? All we really need to do is simply knock on the door, inhale, exhale, say yes, hold the vision of what we are endeavoring to achieve and wait for the door to open. Then we should tell ourselves, "I surrender to my highest good and trust that everything comes to me at the right time, in the right way" and wait for further insight. There is no need to barge in, no need to break down doors. All we have to do is to ask the doors of opportunities to open, be patient, and then take the next step. Meditation provides insight on what steps to take.

And what if, perchance, the door does not open? Here is the best part: So what? There are infinite numbers of doors out there. We will find a new door and create another opportunity. We are the architects of our lives!

Sometimes doors merely lead to hallways, and the hallways lead to the destination. So if that door is not opening, maybe that particular door is simply a hallway, a tactic, a *how* that needs adjusting. We must keep our minds fixed on our *what*, the result, and let the Universe work out the details. When we say yes to our visions, our *what*, and relinquish the *how*, the Universe will find another way for us, and we will be prepared to embrace it. Every locked door is an opportunity for recovery, an opportunity for your new creation.

Therefore, go forth into your life creating. You have limitless possibilities once you realize your body, your mind, your Soul, and your life are of your own design. Release resistance. Embrace responsibility. Make deliberate choices to fully inhabit your life in the best way possible, in harmony with yourself and with the world. Care for your physical body. Meditate. Nurture your Soul. Find a teacher. Be a student. Embrace your own nature and become your owner Master Teacher. Life is a heartbeat of ups and downs. You can recover from the downs. You have the tools. You are the architect. *Now* is the time.

ACKNOWLEDGMENTS

MY HEARTFELT THANKS goes to John "Yanni" Alexiou, Lynn Braz, Jason Campbell, Susan and Ronald Rubin, Fred Lublin, M.D., Thalia Alexiou, Kriss Stavrinos, Maciej Poltorak, M.D., and Frank Sabina who helped me transform my life and make this book a reality. Thank you to Alex Cena, the first professional photographer to photograph my postures and capture in pictures the beauty of the yoga I felt within. I have immense gratitude and appreciation for everyone at Steamtown Yoga and for every student I've had the pleasure and honor to teach and inspire, and who, ultimately, taught and inspired me. Thank you to all my teachers who shared their knowledge and insight with me over the years, especially Master Jason Campbell, Master Michael Leone, Master Ping Chen, Jimmy Barkan, and Bikram Choudhury. I am grateful for my first Hot Yoga teacher Carolan Sudol who inspired me to attend teacher training and gave me my first teaching opportunity at her Washington, D.C. studio.

ABOUT THE AUTHOR

LARA ALEXIOU COMPLETED her first Yoga Teacher Training Program in 2003 with Bikram Choudhury. Since then, she has trained extensively in yoga, qigong, meditation, and Taoist philosophy with Jimmy Barkan and Zen Wellness. In addition to running her studio, Steamtown Yoga, she is a Zen Business Mentor with Zen Business Mastery, and coaches other studio owners in creating sustainable yoga businesses. She was the 2005 Mid-Atlantic Regional Women's Yoga Champion, and competed nationally in 2006. Lara has presented workshops for Yoga Alliance, Mindbody BOLD, The National Qigong Association, and Zen Business Bootcamp LIVE.

You can view her TEDx Talk, Architecture of the Body, Mind, and Soul, by visiting https://youtu.be/-I6UD2q7X2Q. For more information and to read Lara's other yoga and wellness blog, visit her online at steamtownhotyoga.com, and follow her on social media: @laraalexiou.

Made in the USA
Middletown, DE
14 July 2017